# A Handbook for Classical Lutheran Education

*The Best of The Consortium for Classical and Lutheran Education's Journals*

*Edited by:*

Steven A. Hein, Cheryl Swope

Paul J. Cain, Tom Strickland

# A Handbook for Classical Lutheran Education

*The Best of The Consortium for Classical and Lutheran Education's Journals*

The Consortium for Classical and Lutheran Education www.ccle.org

# Contents

Soli Deo Gloria

# Foreword

*by Gene Edward Veith*

This volume is a handbook on Classical Lutheran Education. It explains what it is and why it is needed today. It shows the importance of classical education to Western civilization in general and to the Lutheran tradition in particular. It explains how to teach using this educational approach, including how to teach particular subjects (e.g., music, history, English, writing). It also suggests ways that a classical curriculum can be implemented in different contexts, such as in homeschooling, homeschool/parochial school hybrids, and special education.

These articles are gleaned from two journals published by the Consortium for Classical and Lutheran Education. *The Classical Education Quarterly* was published from 2007-2009, under the editorship of Dr. Steven Hein. This journal changed its name to The Classical Lutheran Education Journal and became an annual publication when Kathrine E. Bischof and Cheryl Swope took on the editorial duties from its first issue in 2010. Cheryl later continued as the journal's editor with Dr. Hein, and she continues today. Most of the articles, in turn, have been based on presentations to the CCLE conferences held annually, except for two years, since 1999.

The current rediscovery of classical Christian education began in the 1980s with efforts to implement the trivium of grammar, logic, and rhetoric according to the developmental model set forth by Dorothy L. Sayers in her essay "The Lost Tools of Learning." Since then, as reflected in these essays, the classical education movement has deepened its understanding of the liberal arts, seeing in the arts of the *trivium* a conceptual model for all of learning, as well as illuminating subjects in themselves. Meanwhile, other treasures of the classical educational tradition have been brought back to light. In addition to the language arts of the trivium are the mathematical arts of the *quadrivium* (arithmetic, geometry, music, and astronomy). The *Progymnasmata* was a method of teaching writing—and creativity—to young children. The skills of the seven liberal arts were employed in the realms of knowledge classified as the three sciences of the classical tradition (natural science, moral science, and theological science).

This fuller picture of the liberal arts tradition is in contrast to the truncated version of the "liberal arts" that we see invoked by so many colleges, in which "the liberal arts" simply means "the humanities" or "courses that are not vocational." Recently, there have been calls for jettisoning the liberal arts in favor of the more marketable subjects of Science, Technology, Engineering, and Mathematics. But this is simply the progressive educator's definition of the liberal arts, making them into just another academic specialty among many others. The actual liberal arts—that is, the liberal arts of classical education—comprised a comprehensive educational philosophy and methodology capable of teaching virtually anything in a thorough, effective way. Four of the seven liberal arts were all about mathematics, and, as Dr. Christian Kopff shows us in these pages and elsewhere, classical education essentially gave us modern science.

The distinction between "liberal" education and "vocational" training has a better pedigree, going back through Cardinal John Henry Newman through medieval scholasticism to Aristotle, and yet it too poses a false dichotomy. The recognition that some things are valuable in themselves, whereas other things are valuable because they lead to other good things, is helpful. Things that are good, true, or beautiful do not have to be used for other ends—such as making money from them—despite the pragmatism of our contemporary culture. Knowing a fact of history or being able to think through a moral issue or experiencing a beautiful piece of music are worthy goals of education, whether or not such knowledge leads to a "job." Looming behind Aristotle is the Greek and Roman distinction between an education for a free citizen (the word for which gives us "liberal") and the education for a slave (a "servile" education). The purpose of a liberal arts education has been the formation of a free citizen. And yet, Aristotle denigrated "service" as unfitting for a free individual. (Aristotle, 1997, p. 138) The Aristotelian notion that "leisure," rather than labor, is the highest goal of human life would manifest itself in the monasticism of the scholastics, with the exaltation of the "contemplative" life over the "active" life. This also shaped the version of classical education practiced by the medieval universities.

Here we see the value of Classical *Lutheran* education. Not only did Luther and Melanchthon reform the medieval universities according to the Renaissance appropriation of the liberal arts, emphasizing the art of rhetoric, with its creativity and its use of original sources (such as the Bible). Luther also recovered the doctrine of vocation, the teaching that God calls, equips, and works through individual human beings in their diverse roles in the economic order, the family, the church, and the state. The purpose of all of these vocations—most of which were repudiated by monastic vows—is the purpose of the Christian life on earth; namely, to love and serve our neighbors. As evident here in Rev. John Hill's extremely helpful article "Luther on Classical Education" and in Dr. Steven Hein's profound treatment "The Freedom of Grace and the Bondage of the Neighbor," classical education is vocational education. Not in the narrow sense of training for a job—though classical education helps its students cultivate all of their God-given talents, including what they may someday use to make a living—but in the sense of equipping them for service. From a Lutheran perspective, the "liberal" in "the liberal arts" points to Christian freedom, which comes from the Gospel of Christ and the Calling received in Baptism, which manifest themselves in the love of God as expressed in love and service to the neighbor.

Thomas Korcok, in his book *Lutheran Education*, reviewed in this volume, defines the Lutheran educational tradition as simply the liberal arts plus catechesis. (Korcok, 2011, p. 61) He also shows the continual importance for Lutheran schools of Baptism and Vocation. (Korcok, 2011, pp. 42-47) All of this is evident in today's classical Lutheran Schools, in parishes and in homes, in the programs and publications of the Consortium for Classical and Lutheran Education, and in the pages of this book.

---

**Dr. Gene Edward Veith** received his B.A. in Letters (Literature, Philosophy, History, and Classics) from the University of Oklahoma and his M.A. and Ph.D. in English from the University of Kansas. He serves as Provost and Professor of Literature at Patrick Henry College. The Director of the Cranach Institute at Concordia Theological Seminary in Ft. Wayne, Indiana, he is the author of over 100 scholarly articles and 18 books on topics involving classical education, Christianity and culture, literature, and the arts. His books include *Classical Education, Loving God with All Your Mind, God at Work, Postmodern Times, and Reading Between the Lines.* He and his wife, Jackquelyn, have three grown children and eight grandchildren. Dr. Veith is Founding Member and permanent Board member of the Consortium for Classical and Lutheran Education.

## About The Consortium for Classical and Lutheran Education

**The Consortium for Classical and Lutheran Education** encourages and serves families, teachers, and schools working to restore the classical arts of learning and the best traditions of Lutheran education.

The CCLE cultivates this restoration through educational conferences, online resources for teachers and parents, and accreditation for classical Lutheran schools. We heartily agree with Martin Luther that "You parents can provide your children with no greater gift than an education in the liberal arts." The Consortium's goal is to give every family the opportunity and tools to follow Luther's advice.

A liberal arts education . . . the arts of classical learning . . . classical education all refer to the same tradition that has been the standard of excellence in education for more than 2000 years. To the ancient Greeks and to the Romans following in their footsteps, this was the only sort of education worthy of a free man, hence the term *liberales artes*, literally "the arts of freedom."

It was a return to this classical learning that fueled the Reformation and the Renaissance. Martin Luther, Philip Melanchthon, and Johann Sturm fostered and guided that restoration in the sixteenth century setting up schools that became the pattern and model for hundreds of years in the western world cultivating wisdom, eloquence, and piety.

Today, the CCLE is working for the restoration of this inheritance among Lutheran schools and educators.

> *So it was done in ancient Rome. There boys were so taught that by the time they reached their fifteenth, eighteenth, or twentieth year they were well versed in Latin, Greek, and all the liberal arts (as they are called), and then immediately entered upon a political or military career. Their system produced intelligent, wise, and competent men, so skilled in every art and rich in experience that if all the bishops, priests, and monks in the whole of Germany today were rolled into one, you would not have the equal of a single Roman soldier. As a result their country prospered; they had capable and trained men for every position. So at all times throughout the world simple necessity has forced men, even among the heathen, to maintain pedagogues and schoolmasters if their nation was to be brought to a high standard.*
> - Martin Luther

Notes

# I. Classical Lutheran Education: Introductory Essays

Notes

# The Case for Resurrecting Classical Education

*by Dr. Steven A. Hein*

When we ponder the kind of education that the next generation in the Church will need for a responsible walk of faith in the Church and in the world, it could be said for parents and for Christian educators, *we are really up against it.* How are we to get the job done with so many elements in our environment working against us? Much of contemporary culture and the trends of progressive education seem to offer less and less in the way of needed resources. Indeed, they have become a major part of the problem. Let's face it. Neither the presuppositions of Christianity nor even those of the once-popular rationalistic naturalism have much impact on the tenor and ethos of contemporary culture. It might well be said, as we have begun a new millennium, we seem poised to preside over the collapse of Western civilization as it has existed for 1500 years. The problem for the Church and its citizens is not simply that Christian truth and its power to shape our culture has evaporated; the real challenge is that much of Western culture has ended its belief in, and commitment to, any rational understanding and ordering of what could be considered true, or good, or beautiful. Pessimism about absolutes reigns supreme in our contemporary post-modern culture.

But this is not even the half of it. Today our young people - yes even those baptized in the Lord - are being bombarded with two powerful forces shaping their lives and identities. The first of these, ironically, is something that once was an ally to education and enlightenment: information. Today information has become an enormous threat. With the advent of the computer and the information highway of the Internet, a numbing information explosion is taking place in all sectors of our lives. Information, once a friend, has now turned against us as a commodity to be purchased and used as one chooses. It can be utilized as a form of entertainment or as a style of dress for status. And it is! Moreover, the connection between information and action has been severed.

Yet the biggest problem today is that we haven't a clue how to determine what information is true or important. Neil Postman made the point in his definitive essay, "Informing Ourselves to Death" (Postman, 1990) that *in a world without spiritual or intellectual order, nothing is unbelievable, nothing predictable and therefore nothing comes as a particular surprise.* We are free to believe or disbelieve most anything today *because we no longer have a comprehensive or consistent picture of the world which would make any claim or alleged fact appear as an unacceptable contradiction. We believe, asserts Postman, because there is no reason not to believe. No social, political, historical, metaphysical, logical or spiritual reason. We live in a world that, for the most part, makes no sense to us.*

The more we cloak ourselves in technological glory, yes even the development of the computer and the explosion of information, the more the human dilemma is as it has always been: "How can we conduct successful inquiries into what is true, good, and beautiful so that we might acquire the things that we need for the world's fight and the soul's salvation?" Here is where we are up against it. For although equipping learners to carry out such inquiries has been the primary task of education shaped by Christian worldview, contemporary culture which has despaired of the existence of such absolutes has turned the task of education and its resources into programs of self-esteem, cultural assimilation, and pleasant experiences that train for secure and lucrative jobs.

The second powerful force that is affecting all levels of education, both in the secular world and in the Church, is our contemporary cultural ethos which is absorbed with personal consumption and entertainment. Mark Edmundson of the University of Virginia has typified the general state of affairs of the American higher education as *Lite Entertainment for Bored College Students*. He writes that the "university culture, like American culture at large, is, to put it crudely, ever more devoted to consumption and entertainment, to the using and using up of goods and images." (Edmundson, 1997) Education must be made fun and entertaining. The central goal of education for so many students today is to acquire a good job and make lots of money for the purpose of even greater entertainment and consumption.

Schools are not marketing rigorous academics these days; rather they are appealing to students on the basis of how many facilities they have for leisure activities and entertainment - refurbished student unions, sports complexes, and the like. Edmundson put it this way: *before they arrive, we ply the students with luscious ads, guaranteeing them a cross between summer camp and lotusland. When they get here, flattery and nonstop entertainment are available, if that's what they want.* (Edmundson, 1997) And what should be said of the academics? There has been a progressive dumbing-down in grading and an ever-increasing number of choices for courses a student would take in his individual programs and fewer standard required courses. Don't like a course or would you like to blow it off? No problem. You can take the class pass/fail or drop it even up to two weeks from the end of the term with nothing but a "W" showing on your transcript.

It is into this culture and this state of progressive education today that the voice of an alternative has been increasingly raised among disgruntled educators and parents both inside and outside of the Church. When the call for a classical approach to education is sounded, this is not simply another experimental program being advocated in the name of educational reform. Classical education is not a gimmick, nor is it a reforming movement within contemporary educational circles. The call for the classical approach to education is a call for an educational renaissance. It is a call to return to the well-established educational goals, methods, and strategies that flourished in Western civilization for over 2000 years and in this country as well, until about 75 to 100 years ago.

Classical education's methods and strategies are different in significant ways from those of the progressive model because its character and goals are different. The goal of classical education is to raise up a virtuous educated person who knows in a normative way himself, his world, and his God. This virtue is grounded in the righteousness of faith and Christian maturity. It is anchored in the Christian virtues of faith, hope, and love, but also includes the worldly virtues: wisdom, courage, temperance, prudence, and chastity. Classical education at its core is normative education. It seeks answers to questions about the meaning, purpose, and value of things. Whereas contemporary progressive education has limited learning largely to analysis, quantitative distinctions, and causal relations within a naturalistic framework (having no interest in first or final causes), classical education seeks to explore the meaning, purposes, and value of knowledge. Classical education believes that learning is shallow and ultimately boring when it is not able to ask questions and receive truthful answers especially about the ultimate issues of human existence: What is life? What is death? And, how can we secure the future?

Today's post-modern education drowns the learner in a cultural relativism, insisting that language simply connects with meaning and usage, not the truth of how things actually are. Quantitative analysis governs all scientific questions, as if this kind of inquiry yields all the information that can be known, or simply all the information that is worth knowing. Such inquiries acquaint the learner with sterile dissected pieces, parts and quantities connected by intermediate causal relationships. For instance, contemporary science deals only with questions of the intermediate causalities of how water moves from a liquid to a crystalline solid state that is less dense – ice floats. The more interesting questions of meaning and teleology are ignored as unscientific. Unlike most all other molecular compounds, why does water move to a less dense state when it becomes a solid? Why does ice float and water freeze from the top down? Answer: to preserve marine life.

Classical education engages an extended conversation among students, instructors, and the great thinkers and writers of the past and present. It nurtures students to become efficient, effective, life-long learners. In this sense, the task of education according to the classical model is to liberate the learner from formal education and instruction. It is to equip the learner with the fundamental skills and arts to enable independent, significant inquiries into knowledge – especially to ask questions and find answers about the meaning, purpose, and value of things. A classical education nurtures the basic language skills necessary to determine what is true, what is good, and what is beautiful on more profound and comprehensive levels. This equipping begins at the earliest levels of education.

The ancients believed that there were seven skills or arts that an educated person needed to be an effective, efficient learner. In the Middle Ages these skills were divided into three primary skills of learning *(The Trivium)* and four secondary *(The Quadrivium)*. The three primary language skills are of central concern on the primary and secondary levels of education. They involve a three-part process of training the mind's facility and use of grammar, logic (or dialectics), and rhetoric. These language skills exist in a logical, building-block relationship with one another. Teaching these skills works best when instructional strategies are employed at stages of intellectual maturity when children have the greatest interest and ability to learn them. The early years of school are spent in absorbing facts, systematically laying the foundations for advanced study. In the middle grades, students learn to think through arguments. In the high school years, they learn to express themselves. This classical pattern is called the *Trivium*. The word *Trivium* and its close associate *Trivia* do not mean what is often implied by them today. Indeed, something that is *trivial* is foundational, not insignificant. *Tri* (three) and *Via* (way) reference the foundational three ways of learning with the use of language. Grammar, logic, and rhetoric - the basic language learning skills - are what Dorothy Sayers has called in her most influential essay, *The Lost Tools of Learning.* (Sayers, 1947)

The first years of schooling are best concentrated on what is called The *grammar stage* of learning. Here the concentration is on language. Language is the operating system of the mind and the means of communication written and oral. One's ability to think and speak cannot rise in depth or complexity above one's facility with language. Knowledge and skill with language are the building blocks for all other learning, just as grammar is the foundation for language.

Ideally, in the elementary school years – what we commonly think of as grades one through four – the mind is best ready to absorb information. Children at this age actually find memorization easy and fun. So during this period, education involves not self-expression and self-discovery as is common in progressive education strategies, but rather the learning of facts. Children learn rules of phonics and spelling, rules of grammar, poetry, the vocabulary of foreign languages, the stories of history and literature, descriptions of plants and animals and the human body, the facts of mathematics – the list goes on. This information makes up the "grammar" or the basic building blocks for all higher forms of knowledge and education. On the level of Grammar, instruction is direct. The instructor carries out the role in education as a lecturer who provides the needed information and facts, terminology, history, and structures of whatever is being learned. A student learns the foundations and language of history, of anatomy, of geography, etc. But just hearing or reading the information is not enough. It must be committed to memory in order to be internalized. Here students work to make the grammar their own.

The teacher functions as a coach who supervises practice, devises drills, motivates performance, and works one-on-one for mastery. In three words the grammar stage is digested – Memorize! Memorize! Memorize!

In the middle grades, a child's mind begins to think more analytically. Middle-school students are less interested in finding out facts than in asking "Why?" The second phase of the classical education, *the logic stage*, is a time when the child begins to pay attention to cause and effect, to the relationships between different fields of knowledge, to the way facts fit together into a meaningful framework. A student is ready for the Logic Stage when the capacity for abstract thought begins to mature. During these years, the student begins algebra and the study of logic. He begins to apply critical thinking to all academic subjects. The logic of writing, for example, includes paragraph construction and learning to support a thesis; the logic of reading involves the criticism and analysis of texts, not simple absorption of information; the logic of history demands that the student find out why the War of 1812 was fought, rather than simply reading its story; the logic of science requires that the child learn inductive reasoning.

The final skill of a classical education is rhetoric. *The rhetoric stage* builds on the skills of grammar and logic. At this point, the high school student learns to write and speak with force and originality. Here the student does more than memorize or analyze what others have contributed to the conversation in the inquiry into knowledge; instead, here the student joins the conversation and offers his own contributions. The student of rhetoric applies the rules of logic learned in middle school to the foundational information learned in the early grades and expresses his conclusions, applications, and evaluations in clear, persuasive language.

A classical education is more than simply a pattern of learning, though. Classical education is language-focused; learning is accomplished primarily through words, written and spoken, rather than an emphasis on images (pictures, videos, and television). Why is this important? Language-learning and image-learning require very different habits of thought. Language requires the mind to work harder; in reading, the brain is forced to translate a symbol (words on the page) into a concept. Images, such as those on videos and television, allow the mind to be passive. In front of a video screen, the brain can "sit back" and relax, but faced with the written page, the mind is required to be intensely active.

A classical education, then, has two important learning aspects. It follows a specific three-part pattern of learning and it is language-focused. The mind must be first supplied with facts, then given the logical tools for organization of knowledge, and finally equipped to express conclusions. Moreover, in the classical model, all knowledge is understood as interrelated. Astronomy (for example) is not studied in isolation; it is learned along with the history of scientific discovery, which leads into the church's relationship to science and from there to the intricacies of medieval church history. The reading of the Odyssey leads the student into the consideration of Greek history, the nature of heroism, the development of the epic, and man's understanding of the divine.

A classical education integrates most ideally by using history as its organizing outline – beginning with the ancients and progressing forward to the moderns in history, science, literature, philosophy, religion, art and music. The classical model is highly systematic, in direct contrast to the scattered, unorganized nature of so much primary and secondary education. Systematic and rigorous study has two purposes. First, such study develops virtue in the student. Aristotle defined virtue as the ability to act in accordance to what one knows to be right. The virtuous man (or woman) can force himself to do what he knows to be right, even when it runs against his inclinations. Classical education continually asks a student to work against his baser inclinations (laziness or the desire to watch another hour of TV) in order to reach a goal – mastery of a subject.

Systematic study also allows the student to join what Mortimer Adler calls the Great Conversation – the ongoing conversation of great minds down through the ages. In contrast, progressive education has become so eclectic that the student has little opportunity to make meaningful connections between past events and the flood of current information. The beauty of the classical curriculum, writes classical schoolmaster David Hicks, *is that it dwells on one problem, one author, or one epoch long enough to allow even the youngest student a chance to exercise his mind in a scholarly way: to make connections and to trace developments, lines of reasoning, patterns of action, recurring symbolisms, plots, and motifs.* (Hicks, 1999, p. 133)

With this educational model, the need to prepare students for cultural assimilation and a good job gives way to a curriculum, learning strategies, and goals that will provide an education for the making of a life; raising up a competent life-long learner who is in touch with the God who saves, the world that He has created, and a virtuous walk of faith that He has called us to live. Students of this kind of education become equipped to deal with the most pressing issues of human existence: *the world's fight and the soul's salvation.* (Hicks, 1999, p. 2) The learner will have some knowledge and a growing appreciation and passion for truth, goodness, and beauty. We seek an education that, in the words of Cardinal Newman, teaches the student *to see things as they are, to go right to the point, to disentangle a skein of thought, to detect what is sophistical, and to discard what is irrelevant. It prepares him to fit any post with credit, and to master any subject with facility.* (Newman, 2005, p. 152)

---

Dr. Steven Hein is an affiliate faculty member at Patrick Henry College. Founding member of the Consortium for Classical and Lutheran Education, he serves as Director of the Concordia Institute for Christian Studies.

Notes

## Latin and the Lutheran Reform of the Medieval Curriculum

*by Dr. E. Christian Kopff*

When the worst of the Dark Ages was past, Charlemagne (742-814) strove to restore order and empire in Europe. He turned to England for scholars and teachers such as Alcuin (735-814) to re-establish classical education. The old schools had disappeared, so monasteries and cathedrals were encouraged to found schools, modeled on the one at Charlemagne's court. The neo-Platonic ideal of the Seven Liberal Arts, known from Augustine and Martianus Capella, was the basis of the curriculum. The cultural triumphs of the Latin Middle Ages were based on a curriculum that was the product of late ancient speculation taught at monasteries and cathedrals - institutions that did not exist in pagan culture - and carried on in Latin, a "dead" language without native speakers. In practice, pride of place went to grammar, the study of Latin language and literature leading to the reading of the Two Canons, the biblical and secular (pagan) Great Books. Logic and rhetoric, the rest of the trivium, in second place, were often taught more rigorously than the quadrivium (arithmetic, music, geometry and astronomy). Whatever its limitations, this curriculum was a true core with a reading list of Great Books and a balance between the study of language and that of mathematics and science. As culture and commerce recovered, universities arose to teach professional subjects, such as law, medicine, and theology, which were soon joined by the arts in the wider sense, including philosophy.

The institutional basis of this curriculum was shaken by the Reformation. By 1524 Martin Luther (1483-1546) and his brilliant young Humanist friend and colleague Philip Melanchthon (1497-1560) were worried. The Reformation proclamation of Christian Freedom had turned into an excuse for license and a wholesale rejection of tradition. Cloisters were shut and their schools were closed. Erasmus wrote scornfully, "Ubicunque regnat Lutheranismus, ibi litterarum est interitus." ("Wherever Lutheranism reigns, there is the death of culture.")

Martin Luther had always been a strong supporter of a liberal arts education. In his important open letter "To the Christian Nobility of the German Nation" (1520) Luther urged reforming the universities and emphasized the importance of teaching Latin, Greek, and Hebrew. He proclaimed his commitment to liberal education by writing to Humanist Eobanus Hessus, "Without knowledge of literature, pure theology cannot endure. In the recent past, when letters were weak and fell, so did theology....There has never been a great revelation of God's Word unless He has first prepared the way by the rise and prosperity of languages and letters." In 1524 Luther called upon local governments to found public schools in *An die Brgermeister und Ratsherrn alle Stdte in deutschen Landen, dass sie christliche Schulen aufrichten und halten sollen,* ("A Letter to the Councilmen of all the Cities in Germany, Urging Them to Found and Maintain Christian Schools"). He had heard the objections to the classical curriculum that contemporary classical educators still hear, "If we must have schools, why teach Latin, Greek, Hebrew and the other liberal arts? Is it not enough to teach the Scriptures in our mother tongue?" He answered firmly, "If the languages were of no practical benefit, they are still wonderful gifts from God," but "the languages are the scabbard in which the sword of the Spirit is sheathed." He took his case to lay people in his famous "Sermon to Parents, On Sending their Children to School" in 1530.

While Luther was writing and preaching in favor of a liberal arts education that emphasized language and literature, Melanchthon was in charge of the institutional side of curricular reform. He began visiting German cities to observe and advise them on education. In 1528 he published the *Visitation Articles,* his considered judgment as scholar and teacher on standards for schools.

The first part was a statement of faith. The three parts of a Christian life are repentance in response to the Law, followed by faith in the Gospel from which flows a life of good works. For those good works, however, education is needed. So the second part of the Visitation Articles was a school plan. Human fulfillment in this life is based on language, to be learned by studying the traditional trivium: Latin grammar, logic and rhetoric. For Melanchthon the best education concentrates on a few basic subjects.

Elementary education was in the truest sense grammar school, and the grammar was Latin grammar. First children learned their letters, the Creed, and the Lord's Prayer. Then they studied Donatus' Latin grammar and the traditional wise sayings of Cato. Basic Latin vocabulary and grammar were emphasized. When they had mastered these, students went on to read Aesop's Fables and the Latin Colloquies of Erasmus, and they studied music. A solid grounding in grammar was essential for the success of this curriculum. "If such labor is irksome to the teacher, as we often see, then we should dismiss him and hire one who will not shirk his duty, which is keeping his pupils attentive to grammar. No greater injury can befall learning and the arts than for young people to grow up ignorant of grammar," Melanchthon wrote. The reward for mastering grammar was reading the Bible and the pagan classics: Cicero, Virgil and Ovid. Greek was taught chiefly to read the New Testament, but some schools taught Isocrates, Homer, and Greek tragedy such as Euripides' Hecuba. The Two Canons, the Great Books curriculum of Late Antiquity, were still fundamental but now supplemented by the Greek New Testament and a few Greek secular authors.

Melanchthon's curricular model spread across northern Europe through the influence of men such as Johannes Sturm (1507-1589) in Strasburg and Johannes Bugenhagen (1485-1558) in Germany and Scandinavia. By the second half of the 16th century it flourished in England, where the evidence is presented in one of the greatest works of American scholarship, T. W. Baldwin's *William Shakspere's "Small Latine & Lesse Greeke"*. (Baldwin, 1944)

This "grammar school" education provided the foundation for theology, law, medicine, and science in Protestant countries. The Jesuits imitated it in their excellent schools in Catholic lands. Schools with this curriculum graduated Shakespeare and Bacon, Racine and Voltaire, Bach and Handel, Milton and Newton, Thomas Jefferson and John Adams. In the 19th century the English Public School and the German Classical Gymnasium used the same educational ideals and reading list, with somewhat more attention given to Greek. John Keats and Charles Darwin, Karl Marx and Friedrich Nietzsche, Albert Einstein and Werner Heisenberg attended schools with a classical core curriculum. The Reformation's Humanist reform of the medieval liberal arts curriculum created the basis for biblical Christianity and ordered freedom, literary, and scientific creativity for 500 years. Can a curriculum modeled on it produce similar fruits in the 21st century? That is the challenge that inspires contemporary American classical educators.

---

Dr. E. Christian Kopff, author of *The Devil Knows Latin: Why America Needs the Classical Tradition*, serves as associate professor of classics in the Honors program at the University of Colorado – Boulder.

## No Hidden Curriculum: Classical Lutheran Education

*by Rev. Stephen Kieser*

"Hidden curriculum," a term that boasts recent intrusion into educational jargon, expresses the idea that schools are busy doing more than teaching an assigned, premeditated, and stated curriculum. To explore a school's hidden curriculum is to delve into the basic values and presuppositions that under gird the educational endeavor but that have not necessarily been identified by those who teach and administrate. A school's hidden curriculum includes social implications, political underpinnings, cultural influences, and even theological assumptions of every activity in an educational setting.

"Hidden curriculum" might also be understood as "worldview," applied to education. James Nickel in *Mathematics: Is God Silent?* has suggested that a *worldview is a network of presuppositions not authenticated by the procedures of natural science, a perspective through which everything in human experience is interpreted and human reason is guided... these presuppositions are the filters through which every aspect of knowledge and the experiences of life are understood and interconnected.* (Nickel, 2001) Those interested in hidden curriculum ask questions such as: What presuppositions are active in the learning process? How can these presuppositions be detected? What specific actions or rituals are adhered to by those with specific presuppositions? Are the presuppositions beneficial to the educational task?

The concept of hidden curriculum has been applied to education in different ways by such notables such as John Dewey, Phillip Jackson, Benson Snyder, Michael Harlambos, and John Taylor Gatto. For example, while Dewey used the idea to promote his pro-democratic perspectives in *Democracy and Education* (Dewey, 2010), Gatto used the same concept to radically criticize compulsory education in his book *Dumbing Us Down: The Hidden Curriculum of Compulsory Schooling.* (Gatto, 1992) Thought to be discovered primarily through the scientific process, the hidden curriculum must be discerned through evaluation of all concrete forms. These may include teaching methodologies, student-to-teacher and teacher-to-student verbal and non-verbal interactions (or lack thereof), and curricular resources employed or avoided. The goal is to decode from what is observable values, attitudes, presuppositions - the worldview - transmitted to the learner, often unintentionally by the teacher or school system.

While attending a synodical college as an undergraduate student desiring to teach in a Lutheran school, I was drilled in the concept of hidden curriculum. Later, while earning my administrator's endorsement from another synodical college, I encountered the topic again in a similarly rigorous fashion. We were taught various strategies in identifying the hidden curriculum. The primary strategy was teacher observation. The idea was that if a teacher could be observed by an "unbiased" outsider (is that really possible?), he might become aware of habits and activities rooted in specific presuppositions he would have been unable to identify through self-awareness. Then came the arduous task of determining which presuppositions those actions implied. Interestingly, certain teacher activities were already presupposed as negative and others as positive. The evaluation process obviously had its own hidden curriculum!

So what about the inherent, implied, or presupposed meaning of an action? Do actions have meaning apart from context or language? Is every action understood the same way by all who observe it? During a recent lecture on liturgics, the speaker suggested that every action (or ritual form) has its own meaning apart from language and context. To prove his point, he recounted how a pastor had the ritual of taking a newly baptized baby and lifting it silently in the direction of the altar. Later, someone asked the pastor why he offered the baby to God. "Hadn't God already made the child His own possession through the rite of Baptism without the lifting up of the child at the altar?" the parishioner asked. The parishioner understood the action of lifting the baby at the altar to be in conflict with the action of baptizing, as if the parent was now offering the child to God since Baptism did not accomplish the task. When questioned about his ritual, the pastor gave no specific meaning behind why he lifted up the baby, only to say that he had seen it done by another pastor. Using the concept of hidden curriculum, it might be said that the pastor discovered through the observation of a parishioner that his action sent a presupposed - and unintended - message.

Does the action of lifting up the baby at the altar have its own implied meaning apart from language and context? Not necessarily. An action without an assigned meaning may be given one or more meanings by an observer, based on the context and language surrounding the action. It is very possible that if the congregation was to be questioned on the implied meaning of the pastor's action, each member might offer differing meanings. Even if the pastor had a specific meaning that he hoped to convey in lifting up the child, it may not be clear without a spoken or written explanation. Apart from clearly communicating via context and language, actions can be ambiguous. Indeed, action, context, and language serve each other well in the task of communication. Uncontrolled, spontaneous dancing does not convey reverence in worship. A mathematics teacher who shows up to class in a bikini does not convey that she has come prepared to teach fractions. Indeed, an action on its own may not lend itself to convey a specific meaning.

Sometimes, a specific action has a meaning that has been assigned in such an enduring way that to give the action a new meaning may not be possible. In Lutheran circles at one time, it would have been unthinkable to break the host during the administration of the Lord's Supper. Displaying a single middle finger to your students would not be the best action to express the Biblical truth of unity in the Trinity. In reality, a hidden curriculum need not be hidden only to be uncovered through a scientific process. Instead, Lutheran education would be better served by ignoring the current obsession with hidden curriculum.

A better way to proceed is to first determine the worldview and curricular content that is desired and then identify the best actions to accomplish the task. In other words, education ought to be deliberate and focused, not hidden. Rather than proceeding with actions that have, at best, implied meanings, the teacher chooses and deliberately executes predetermined actions or teaching methods to accomplish a well-established, predetermined, and utterly unhidden curriculum.

Thankfully, this educational task is not a new one. Sound, well-established actions have been beautifully linked to an education that has proven itself worthy of repetition and is uniquely Christian: Classical Lutheran Education. The *Consortium for Classical and Lutheran Education* has developed the identifying "Marks of a Lutheran and Classical School." (CCLE, 2010) In this document, the three primary marks are as follows:

1. The school confesses and incorporates a commitment to the Gospel of our Lord Jesus Christ in all aspects of its educational mission as it is taught and confessed in the inspired sacred Scriptures and the confessional writings of the Evangelical Lutheran Church.

2. The school demonstrates a commitment to a classical approach to curriculum and instruction within the framework of its confessional, Lutheran character.

3. The school's institutional governance establishes and expresses clearly articulated rules, regulations, and responsibilities that are in harmony with God's revealed orders of creation – for students, parents, and school staff.

With the worldview intentionally and authentically exposed, there is no guess work as to what teachers and schools must do. Teacher supervision no longer serves as the tool for discovery of the hidden curriculum, but rather a means for determining how well the teacher is implementing the school's clearly articulated worldview. The usefulness of school facilities, opportunities in music, art, and languages; as well as the use of computers and other technology; indeed, everything that happens (or that does not happen), every idea and all decisions are evaluated on whether or not they accomplish the well-articulated, intentional curriculum.

With such a model we begin with stating the "hidden curriculum" of classical and Lutheran education and articulating it so that it is no longer hidden, but clear, concise, and teachable. Theology and the educational task join hands to form the firm foundation from which all actions happen, and instructional methodologies must stand the test of this foundation. Teachers come to their students already aware of which activities are beneficial to learning and how these activities might be used in service to the Gospel for the neighbor's good.

---

The Reverend Stephen Kieser, B.A. Secondary Education from Concordia – Ann Arbor, M.A. Theology from Concordia Theological Seminary, Ft. Wayne, and M.A School Administration from Concordia – River Forest; serves as President of the Consortium for Classical and Lutheran Education. Husband to Julia and homeschooling father of seven, he and his family reside in Indiana where he serves as a Lutheran parish pastor.

Notes

## Classical Lutheran Education: Simply Defined

*by Cheryl Swope*

Dr. Gene Edward Veith has suggested that classical Lutheran education can be defined simply as the liberal arts with Lutheran catechesis. "The liberal arts can equip a child for effective service in the world; catechesis can equip a child for everlasting life." (Korcok, 2011, forward by Veith p. xii) The liberal arts cultivate the student's mind and character with academic rigor, tools for learning, and formative content. Lutheran catechesis instructs and nurtures matters of the soul through the Holy Scriptures, the Lutheran confessions, the liturgy and hymnody. With the Seven Liberal Arts, the three sciences: moral, natural and theological; and the Small Catechism's Six Chief Parts, classical Lutheran education equips for dual citizenship in an earthly kingdom and the heavenly kingdom.

### What Are the Seven Liberal Arts?

The Seven Liberal Arts include the three arts of language (trivium) and the four arts of mathematics (quadrivium). "Liberal" derives from the Latin word for "free," as these arts were designed so free men could think about great ideas for the noble service of others. In contrast, the "servile" arts, an education for slaves, prepare for menial labor. The liberal arts enable an individual to live, to study, to think, and to serve others in any vocation.

### The Arts of Language: The Trivium (3)

*Grammar* – all that is foundational in language

Grammar includes learning letters, reading, and spelling; beautiful penmanship, crafting sentences and paragraphs; developing a rich vocabulary. Grammar is taught in part recitation and by imitation – copying excellent writing of others, reading and hearing good literature - and especially through the study of Latin. The disciplined study of the ordered Latin grammar strengthens the student's mind, offers an appreciation of a great literary heritage, and enhances the knowledge of the student's own native grammar and vocabulary. For thousands of years, Greek has also assisted in teaching the arts of language and providing the foundation for reading classic literary works.

*Logic* – analysis of language

Analytical thinking, discernment, and argumentation comprise Logic. The student of Logic learns to identify false statements and illogical premises, whether in his own thinking or in the assertions of others. Logic helps to organize a student's mind and prepare a student for public discourse. Taught in the early years with simple cause and effect of consequences, such as those found in Aesop's fables and in family life, formal Logic is taught as the student's mind matures.

*Rhetoric* – eloquence, beauty, and persuasion with language

Rhetoric enables the student to write and speak with eloquence. Ancient Roman orator Quintilian urged the modeling of excellent speech even with very young children (*Institutio Oratoria*, Book One). When parents and teachers read poetry aloud, they bring beautiful examples of language to their children. As the student masters the foundational and analytical elements of language, lessons in formal Rhetoric become part of his classical education.

### *The Arts of Mathematics – The Quadrivium (4)*

Sometimes neglected in today's applications of classical education, the Quadrivium is designed to strengthen the child's mind while cultivating in him an appreciation for the patterns and order of the world in which he lives. Through the Quadrivium, as with the Trivium, the teacher's purpose is to incline the child toward that which is significantly true, good, and beautiful. This approach to the Mathematical Arts contrasts with the starkly utilitarian questions, *If I will never use this in my daily life, why learn it? If I will not need this to 'get a job,' why study this at all?* The Quadrivium teaches foundational content with a formative impact on the student himself. The Mathematical Arts - far more than isolated bits of knowledge – command a strong presence in the classical curriculum as follows:

*Discrete quantity or number*

    *Arithmetic* – theory of number

    *Music Theory* – application of the theory of number

*Continuous quantity*

    *Geometry* – theory of space

    *Astronomy* – application of the theory of space (Joseph and McGlinn, 2002)

## What Is Catechesis?

. . . instruction for children and the simple folk. Therefore, in ancient times it was called in Greek catechism (i.e., instruction for children). It teaches what every Christian must know.

Therefore, we must have the young learn well and fluently the parts of the catechism or instruction for children, diligently exercising themselves in them, and keep them busy with these parts. (Luther, 1988, Preface)

## What Are The Six Chief Parts?

Martin Luther's Small Catechism divides the teaching of the historic Christian faith into Six Chief Parts:

```
The Ten Commandments
The Apostles' Creed
The Lord's Prayer

The Sacrament of Holy Baptism
Confession
The Sacrament of the Altar
```

As the child studies each part with explanation, he learns the statements of the Lutheran faith. Consider this example from Luther's explanation of The Apostles' Creed:

The First Article: Creation

> I believe that God has made me and all creatures; that He has given me my body and soul, eyes, ears, and all my members, my reason and all my senses, and still takes care of them.... He richly and daily provides me with all that I need to support this body and life.... All this He does only out of fatherly, divine goodness and mercy, without any merit or worthiness in me. For all this it is my duty to thank and praise, serve and obey Him.

> This is most certainly true.

The Second Article: Redemption

> I believe that Jesus Christ, true God, begotten of the Father from eternity, and also true man, born of the Virgin Mary, is my Lord, who has redeemed me, a lost and condemned person, purchased and won me from all sins, from death, and from the power of the devil; not with gold or silver, but with His holy, precious blood and with His innocent suffering and death, that I may be His own and live under Him in His kingdom and serve Him in everlasting righteousness, innocence, and blessedness, just as He is risen from the dead, lives and reigns to all eternity.

> This is most certainly true.

The Third Article: Sanctification

> I believe that I cannot by my own reason or strength believe in Jesus Christ, my Lord, or come to Him; but the Holy Spirit has called me by the Gospel, enlightened

me with His gifts, sanctified and kept me in the true faith. In the same way He calls, gathers, enlightens, and sanctifies the whole Christian church on earth, and keeps it with Jesus Christ in the one true faith. In this Christian church He daily and richly forgives all of my sins and the sins of all believers. On the Last Day He will raise me and all the dead, and give eternal life to me and all believers in Christ.

This is most certainly true. (Luther, 1988, Third Article)

## The Lutheran Doctrine of Vocation

Parents and teachers can find the task of teaching overwhelming. How can I do all of this? With classical education's emphasis on academic rigor and high levels of structure, teachers may grow weary; however, when we remember the important "why" of classical Lutheran education, the daily "how" can become less burdensome, and we find a growing number of excellent resources to support us in our task.

Parents and teachers can take heart. Remember that God Himself works through us, in spite of our weaknesses, to accomplish His good purposes in our children.

God has chosen to work through human beings, who, in their different capacities and according to their different talents, serve each other....The ability to read God's Word is an inexpressibly precious blessing, but reading is an ability that did not spring fully formed in our young minds. It required the vocation of teachers....By virtue of our creation, our purpose in life is to do good works, which God Himself 'prepared' for us to do. We are 'God's workmanship,' which means that God is at work in us to do the works He intends. (Veith, 2002, pp.14, 38)

## Summary: Classical Lutheran Education

Teach them, first of all, the Ten Commandments, the Creed, the Lord's Prayer, always presenting the same words of the text, so that those who learn can repeat them after you and retain them in the memory....When those whom you are instructing have become familiar with the words of the text, it is time to teach them to understand the meaning of those words.

In all things, let the Scriptures be the chief and the most frequently used reading-book, both in primary and high schools, and the very young should be kept in the gospels. (Luther, 1991)

Classical education develops wisdom, eloquence, and virtue for earthly citizenship; Lutheran catechesis teaches that in Christ alone we obtain righteousness for heavenly citizenship. Classical Lutheran education combines the liberal arts with catechesis to implement the formative benefits of the liberal arts while nurturing the child in the historic Christian faith. Classical Lutheran virtue includes humility, as the child who studies Latin or Greek is not to think of himself more highly than the child who does not have such privileges. Instead, he thanks His heavenly Father for an education given from God's own divine fatherly goodness and mercy.

Classical Lutheran education seeks to cultivate in students self-knowledge, tools for learning, the ability to contemplate great ideas, and an understanding of the world in which he lives - all for the love and service of others. Above all, classical and Lutheran education inclines a child toward truth, goodness, and beauty found fully and eternally in the person and work of Jesus Christ. This is most certainly true.

---

Cheryl Swope, M.Ed., is author of *Simply Classical: A Beautiful Education for Any Child.* She and her husband homeschooled their adopted special-needs twins from infancy through high school with classical Lutheran education. She serves as editor of the Classical Lutheran Education Journal and one the Board for the Consortium for Classical and Lutheran Education.

Notes

# II. Classical Education Throughout History

Notes

## On Christian Doctrine: Rhetoric and Dialectic in St. Augustine's De Doctrina Christiana

*by Dr. James Tallmon*

If it is true that, as Aristotle said, rhetoric is a counterpart of dialectic and ethics, then there should be a relatively discernible point at which dialectic, ethics, and rhetoric all converge. Moreover, discovery of truth is traditionally accepted as one of the ends of dialectical inquiry, and there is a point at which the process of invention entails a sort of rhetorical dialectic. This is an intriguing relationship given the historically rigid, dichotomous treatment of dialectic and rhetoric. Saint Augustine's *De Doctrina Christiana* (Augustine, 1995) serves as a profitable study of that relationship, because Augustine advances a Christian ethical standard, a practical logic (which focuses on the unique challenges of Christian hermeneutics), and a Christian view of eloquence. Does Augustine's combination of those particular elements render *De Doctrina* a rhetoric - or is it a dialectic? If rhetoric is reflected, what type of rhetoric is it: philosophical, practical, formulaic, or a hybrid? A selective textual analysis will provide the necessary means of determining which, if any, of the three components is privileged in Augustine's doctrine for Christian teachers. *This exploration will close with a more general meditation on the place of rhetoric in advancing matters of faith.*

### Textual Analysis

Axiology is the study of relationships between various goods, self, and those things surrounding self. Ethics, for example, is the study of the good implied in the relationship between self and others. Politics studies the good in terms of power relationships, and so on. Augustine's first book takes the shape of an axiology through his initial division of the subject matter into "things" and "signs". In Book One, Augustine clearly proceeds in an axiological fashion as he teaches the reader (and would-be teacher) how one ought to relate to things. In so doing, Augustine asserts that some things are to be used and some are to be enjoyed. More importantly, as Augustine explicates the right relationship between selves (both my self and other selves), he unfolds his ethical doctrine – the doctrine of charity – beginning in chapter XXII.

The doctrine of charity is Augustine's ethical imperative derived from Scripture. We are all obligated to love " . . . that which is equal to us and that which is above us." This twofold love constitutes an ethical standard because " . . . all other loves flow into it . . .". (Augustine, 1995, p. 23) Augustine's elaboration of the way in which charity constitutes an ethical standard is perhaps the most profound statement in *De Doctrina*:

> He lives in justice and sanctity who is an unprejudiced assessor of the intrinsic value of things. He is a man who has an ordinate love: he neither loves what should not be loved nor fails to love what should be loved; he neither loves more what should be loved less, loves equally what should be loved less or more, nor loves less or more what should be loved equally.(Augustine, 1995, p. 23)

In the final analysis, *De Doctrina* is not authored as a profound book, and Augustine swiftly moves to harness his own profundity for practical purposes. Chapter XXXVI (page 30) begins a transition to Book Two which contains Augustine's teaching on the interpretation of Scripture.

> Whoever, therefore, thinks that he understands the divine Scriptures or any part of them so that it does not build the double love of God and of our neighbor does not understand it at all. Whoever finds a lesson there useful to the building of charity ... has not been deceived, nor is he lying in any way. (Augustine, 1995, p. 30)

In this passage Augustine establishes a standard for correct hermeneutics and demonstrates (in rare fashion) the borderland between ethics and dialectic. The ethical rule of charity is utilized as a standard for judging the accuracy of Scriptural interpretation, a dialectical tool for discovering truth.

If Book One can be understood as Augustine's ethical doctrine for Christian teachers, then Books Two and Three can be seen as a practical logic for Christian teachers. Augustine develops just enough of the dialectician's art to aid his readers in their hermeneutic capacity. As mentioned above, Augustine divided his subject matter into a study of things and signs. Book Two begins with an examination of signs and quickly moves to those particular signs most important to the would-be teacher: words. Ambiguities are a major stumbling block to correct interpretation of Scripture so, naturally, Augustine focuses his analysis on techniques for rendering ambiguities more clear.

In chapters XXV-XL, Augustine briefly reviews the "human institutions" of secular education, validating those disciplines useful to the Christian exegete. Book Three is the amplification and direct application to Scripture of the dialectical method Augustine developed in the previous book. He maintains the focus on biblical interpretation by providing examples of his method from Scripture. Book Four is Augustine's treatment of eloquence. He begins with an internal summary and then a disclaimer:

> I must thwart the expectation of those readers who think that I shall give the rules of rhetoric here which I learned and taught in the secular schools. And I admonish them not to expect such rules from me, not that they have no utility, but because, if they have any, it should be sought elsewhere if perhaps some good man has the opportunity to learn them. But he should not expect these rules from me, either in this work or in any other. (Augustine, 1995, p. 118)

Here is Augustine's version of the rather standard disclaimer of a reluctance to associate with the first principles of rhetoric. First, the principles of rhetoric (at least as conceived in the Roman tradition) are indeed elemental and mundane. While much in the way of rich teaching on rhetoric is available, the standard treatment – aimed as it was at schoolboys – is rather superficial. Second, rhetoric's perennial bugaboo is guilt by association. From earliest times rhetoric has been associated with all manner of bombast and sophistry, an unpleasantness that especially prompts Saint Augustine to dissociate himself with rhetoric, at least at first glance. The disclaimer must be understood in the specific context of Augustine's purpose, i.e., he wishes to groom his sheep for their responsibilities as teachers – as opposed to tending a flock of declaimers! Again, Augustine makes eloquence serve his practical ends. Hence comments like: "[T]hose with acute and eager minds more readily learn eloquence by reading and hearing the eloquent than by following the rules of eloquence". (Augustine, 1995, p. 119) Augustine apparently did not find it in the best interest of his pupils to study the depths of any of the several potentially deep topics he treats in *De Doctrina*. However, he does not avoid giving practical guidelines. In much the same way that he provided tools for discovering truth, Augustine now explicates a practical set of stylistic guidelines. For example, on page 123, we find Augustine's doctrine of propriety. That is, "Just as there is a kind of eloquence for youth and another kind for age; that should not be called eloquence which is not appropriate to the person speaking." Of the plain style: "But in all their utterances they should first of all seek to speak so that they may be understood." (Augustine, 1995, p. 133) And so on. Augustine explains the styles appropriate to teaching and why a given style is appropriate to a given teaching situation. Chapter XVIII is an interesting example of Augustine's attempt to extract from Cicero useful guidelines for the Christian teacher. He utilizes the Ciceronian categories of forensic eloquence for his own purposes by contrasting the role (and appropriate style) of teachers to the role and style of lawyers.

Much of Augustine's concern with style can be reduced to exhortations to appropriately adapt both to the audience and to the situation. Consider, for example, the following lines: "But no one should think that it is contrary to theory to mix these three manners; rather, speech should be varied with all types of style in so far as this may be done appropriately. For, when one style is maintained too long, it loses the listener." (Augustine, 1995, p. 158) Augustine closes his treatment of eloquence by stressing the importance of audience-centeredness.

## The Question Of Rhetorical Doctrine In *De Doctrina*

Using the sampling of passages above as evidence for surmising Augustine's rhetorical agenda in *De Doctrina*, we will now return to our earlier questions. We have observed what he did. Now we ask, "is it rhetoric? if so, what sort of rhetoric is it?" It all depends on how we define rhetoric, on the purposes of the author, and on how much latitude we are willing to allow in order to uphold our argument!

*De Doctrina* is, in one sense, simply a handbook for students who plan to teach the Scriptures – a seminary textbook on teaching the Word. As Augustine makes clear from his thesis, the work has two broad divisions: discovering the truth and teaching the truth. Insofar as Augustine's goal is to equip students with only the necessities of their vocation, he avoids writing a detailed text for either section. The tools for discovery are few and the tools for teaching are fewer. Therefore, it would seem that Augustine's treatments of dialectic and eloquence are purposefully sketchy so as to avoid undue encumbrance. It is important to always bear in mind Augustine's practicality. He refuses to over-equip his young pupils. They are his "light brigade."

In another important sense, *De Doctrina* is more than a simple textbook on teaching. No doubt due to his expertise in rhetoric, Augustine saw an opportunity to achieve his purposes in short order. He needed only to acquaint his troops with the rhetorician's art, make a few generalizations from rhetoric to teaching, and they would be off and running the good race, fighting the good fight. However, the choice to utilize rhetoric was not entirely unproblematic. That is why in *De Doctrina*, we observe several instances of Augustine's careful attention to potential abuses of the art. Such caveats include *This is not a full-blown rhetoric; Yes, it is acceptable to glean from pagan authors, but, no, one must not expect to achieve blessedness by the study of pagan authors; Rhetoric has been used for ignoble ends – so beware*; etc. Each of these caveats is interesting, and one could speculate on Augustine's perceptions about the power of rhetoric or the value of secular education, but such are not the questions at hand.

Keeping in mind both Augustine's end (equipping Christian teachers) and the particular fashion in which he construes his means of achieving that end (an ethic + some dialectic + a bit of eloquence), one begins to identify a strong rhetorical undercurrent in *De Doctrina*. Considering the Aristotelian conception of rhetoric in its fullness (that it is a counterpart of both ethics and dialectic), *De Doctrina* is a thoroughly rhetorical approach to equipping Christian exegetes. Augustine brings together enough ethics to establish a rule for hermeneutic purity, enough dialectic to aid in exegesis, and enough Roman eloquence to accomplish his practical aim. In other words, Augustine has pulled together a concise volume that covers the essentials of invention and style without overdosing his pupils on rhetorical theory. It is narrow, limited, practical and "sanctified" for Christian workers, but nonetheless, discernable as a rhetoric. One final question requires our attention.

## The Role Of Rhetoric In Matters Of Faith

Can Christian teaching and preaching, with their emphasis on apodeictic proof, ever be regarded as rhetoric? Augustine writes that when one is speaking to those who ought to do something but who do not wish to do it, "then those great things should be spoken in the grand manner in a way appropriate to the persuasion of their minds." (Augustine, 1995, p. 145) Apparently he felt that persuasion concerning matters spiritual was a viable possibility. The question shifts then to whether or not Augustine was right to think so. I believe he was right. Of course the "proofs" of Christianity are demonstrative (apodeictic) but conversion is the domain of evangelism, not teaching. The distinction between the ministry of the evangelist and that of the teacher is critical to the question at hand. The end of teaching is growth or maturity. Thus "practical Christianity" – principles for individual growth and maturity (many of which come veiled in ambiguity – parable, allegory, etc.) – is the stuff of which sermons are made. Such arguments are not based on apodeictic proof but on case reasoning, explications of moral dilemmas, contingencies, and the like. Christian teachers exhort those who already believe to develop the habit of choosing well (which is maturity, "sanctification," "blessedness" or, to borrow Aristotle's term against Augustine's advice, *eudmonia*). The domain of rhetoric is especially the realm of promoting individual maturity through situated arguments, validated by but not solely based upon, apodeictic claims.

On the other hand, rhetoric should not be made a worship. Perhaps that is the spirit of the question. George Kennedy is correct when he asserts that conversion should be understood as an act of the Spirit, but I prefer to view rhetoric as a tool in the hands of God. I think it not too impious to propose that, through the word and faith, rhetoric somehow helps effuse the conversion (the acceptance of apodeictic claims) of those whom God calls. Finally, in a more general sense, theological questions are multidimensional: they frequently hold together in suspension both categorical and contingent elements. The delicate nature of treating such complex questions underscores the wisdom with which Augustine composed his classic work on Christian teaching, *De Doctrina Christiana*, so many centuries ago.

---

Dr. James Tallmon, B.S. and M.A. in Speech Communication, PhD in Rhetoric and Ethics, has served as writer, speaker, and previous Board member for the Consortium for Classical and Lutheran Education. Formerly the Professor of Rhetoric and Director of Debate at Patrick Henry College, Dr. Tallmon serves as Headmaster and Teacher at Trinity Lutheran School in Cheyenne, Wyoming.

## The Middle Ages and "Untrustworthy Monkish Flapdoodle"

*by Angela Hill*

The Middle Ages are the redheaded stepchild of history. Compared to her illustrious sister of Antiquity, her innovative brother of the Renaissance, or her reasonable sister of the Enlightenment, she is backward, awkward, and superstitious. Redheaded stepchild she may be, even of questionable parentage; however, she made herself a servant to her siblings as she bore the brunt of the barbarian invasions and preserved the family treasures as best she could. This article is an attempt to understand the misfit a little better by examining some of her history.

Much of our classical curriculum is based on the Great Books. Of the eight or so medieval works that usually make "the list," none is in the category of histories. The most commonly known types of medieval writings are theological treatises, such as those by Thomas Aquinas, or romances, such as Chrtien de Troyes' Arthurian legends, but we have at least 25 histories and chronicles that date between A.D. 500 and 1500. Often heavily based on the writings of a previous author, they are not considered to be primary sources the way the *Magna Carta* or some other public document would be. For many years these medieval histories were considered to be "untrustworthy monkish flapdoodle." (Brown, 2007) However, experts in the classics such as C.S. Lewis, R.W. Southern, and Peter Brown would impel us to reexamine the value of these works.

C. S. Lewis, in *The Discarded Image*, provides a perceptive description of medieval man that will help us to understand better the selected histories that follow:

> At his most characteristic, medieval man was not a dreamer nor a wanderer. He was an organiser, a codifier, a builder of systems. . . . Distinction, definition, tabulation were his delight. . . . There is nothing which medieval people liked better, or did better, than sorting out and tidying up.

> They are bookish. They are indeed very credulous of books. They find it hard to believe that anything an old *auctour* has said is simply untrue. And they inherit a very heterogeneous collection of books; Judaic, Pagan, Platonic, Aristotelian, Stoical, Primitive Christian, Patristic. . . . Obviously their *auctours* will contradict one another. They will seem to do so even more often if you ignore the distinction of kinds and take your science impartially from the poets and philosophers; and this is what the medievals very often did in fact though they would have been well able to point out, in theory, that poets feigned. If, under these conditions, one has also a great reluctance flatly to disbelieve anything in a book, then here there is obviously both an urgent need and a glorious opportunity for sorting out and tidying up. All the apparent contradictions must be harmonized... (Lewis, 2004, p. 10)

Lewis lists Thomas Aquinas' *Summa Theologica*, Dante's *Divine Comedy*, and even the medieval *Model of the Universe* as the supreme examples of medieval productivity. So we are to expect in these histories an interest in number and balance as well as frequent references to or borrowing from ancient texts.

## I Gregory of Tours (A. D. 538–594): History of the Franks

Gregory became Bishop of Tours in A.D. 573 and served there until his death. Tours was not some backwater town. Tours was the home of Saint Martin, who would eventually become the patron saint of France and of soldiers. Roman roads and the Loire River made Tours accessible to many visitors, political and religious.

Gregory would have been in a powerful position. Thomas Cahill wrote in *How the Irish Saved Civilization* that bishops owned land and often had to carry out justice. (Cahill, 1995, p. 62) Furthermore, as Christianity is a religion of the written Word, bishops and monks could read and write. (Benedictine monks were to read three hours a day in the summer and two hours a day in the winter.) Cahill wrote that with the fall of Roman order it was often up to the bishop to "'civilize' the ruler, introduce to him diplomatically some elementary principles of justice and good government." (Cahill, 1995) As we read Gregory's *History*, we see that he finds himself in just such a situation.

Each book (chapter) of the *History* begins with a preface, although we seem to be missing the preface to the Fourth Book. Gregory writes as if under protest (there is a classical precedent for this modesty) and we will soon see that he is not completely inept in the art of rhetoric:

> With liberal culture on the wane, or rather perishing in the Gallic cities, there were many deeds being done both good and evil: the heathen were raging fiercely; kings were growing more cruel; the church, attacked by heretics, was defended by Catholics; while the Christian faith was in general devoutly cherished, among some it was growing cold; the churches also were enriched by the faithful or plundered by traitors—and no grammarian skilled in the dialectic art could be found to describe these matters either in prose or in verse; and many lamenting and saying: "Woe to our day, since the pursuit of letters has perished from among us and no one can be found among the people who can set forth the deeds of the present on the written page." Hearing continually these complaints and others like them I (have undertaken) to commemorate the past, in order that it may come to be the knowledge of the future; and although my speech is rude, I have been unable to be silent as to the struggles between the wicked and the upright; and I have been especially encouraged because, to my surprise, it has often been said by men of our day, that few understand the learned words of the rhetorician but many the rude language of the common people. (Brehaut, 1969, p. 1)

From Gregory's first sentence, we get a sense of the chaos of his times. The liberal arts have always been connected to leisure, and the fighting of the Merovingian kings did not allow for the peacefulness needed for leisure. Kings were indeed "more cruel." Hardly a page goes by in the History where someone is not being boiled, strangled, stabbed, flogged or flayed. Nobody knew from one day to the next who would be in power. Instability was the norm. Gone were the days of the *Pax Romana*, the Roman senator, and the luxury of rhetoric.

Despite the continual bloodshed, Christianity and its own battles against heresy remained. For the medieval, Christianity is the framework upon which all else is nailed. Christ is the One thing in this world that remains constant; all else is fleeting. It is reasonable, therefore, for Gregory to begin his *History* with the Creation account in Genesis and finish with some talk of Judgment Day. His *History* includes important events of the Bible, the lives of the saints, occasionally the significant things done by various

Roman Emperors. Gregory explains his rationale: "Following the order of time we shall mingle together in our tale the miraculous doings of the saints and the slaughters of the nations." (Brehaut, 1969) That is, Gregory structures his history according to the examples set for him by earlier historians, especially Eusebius, and also Severus, Jerome, and Osorius. (Brehaut, 1969) Medieval historians authenticated their works by including the writings of previous authors.

At first glance, Gregory's "mingling" of secular and sacred history appears to be written simply to show his reader the benefits of a Christian life and the dangers of a pagan one. We cannot deny that he wants all readers to be encouraged in the Christian faith by his *History*; however, Guy Halsall, history professor at the University of York, would have us believe that Gregory has a particular audience in mind. (Halsall, 2007) Gregory hopes to persuade the Merovingian kings to put an end to the strife. Halsall's conclusion is based on his meticulous study of Gregory's preface to Book Five.

Halsall suggests that the preface to Book Five, written in a more formal style, was probably written in the particularly violent year of 576 as an exhortation to the Merovingian aristocracy, including Merovech, son of King Chilperic. The *History* itself had ten books which places this preface directly in the middle of the work. (Remember C. S. Lewis's remarks about medieval organization?) Furthermore, the preface is written as a chiasmus! A chiasmus is a rhetorical device where "sections of text mirror each other around a crux, hence the name." (Halsall, 2007) Classical writers used the chiasmus, but it seems more likely that Gregory internalized it through his study of the Scriptures. Halsall points out that St. John begins his Gospel with a chiasmus, "In the beginning was was Word and the Word was with God and the Word was God; this was in the beginning with God." The very center of the phrase is the crux of that statement: *the Word was God.*

Gregory's chiasmus is quite complex. Here Halsall has translated it from Latin and broken it into 17 sections:

1) It tires me to record the diverse civil wars which afflicted the people and kingdom of the Franks: what is worse we now see the beginning of that time of sorrows, which the Lord foretold.

3) The examples of earlier kings who, as soon as they were divided, were immediately killed by their enemies, should have deterred them.

4) As often as the city of cities and head of the whole world destroyed itself in civil wars, once these wars had ceased, it rose again, as if from the ground.

5) If only, O kings, you exercised yourself in those wars in which your relatives exerted themselves, so that peoples, terrified at your peace, should wonder at your might.

6) Remember what Clovis, the source of your victories did, who killed opposing kings, drove out enemy peoples, subjugated their lands, the rule of which he left to you, safe, sound, and in tact.

7) And when he did this he had neither gold nor silver such as there is now in your treasuries.

8) What are you doing? What do you seek? What do you not have in abundance?

9) In your houses luxuries are in superabundance; wine, wheat and oil abound in your storehouses; gold and silver are heaped up in your treasuries.

10) You lack one thing, that, in not having peace, you are wanting in the grace of God.

11) Why does one man steal things that belong to another? Why does yet another covet things which aren't his?

12) Beware of that [saying] of the Apostle: If you bite and devour one another, take care lest you be consumed by each other.

13) Study old writings carefully and you will see what civil wars produce.

14) Look up what Orosius wrote about the Carthaginians; when he told of the overthrow of their city and territory after 700 years, he added: what served them so long? Concord. What destroyed them after so much time? Discord.

15) Beware of discord, beware of civil wars, which are wiping you and your people out.

16) What else can be expected, other than that, when your army has fallen, left without solace and overthrown by opposing peoples, you should immediately be ruined?

17) If civil war pleases you, O king, exercise that which the apostle reminds us acts within men, so that spirit should strive against flesh (Gal. 5:17), and vices fall before virtues, and that you, who formerly served the root of all evil (Timothy 6:10) in chains, should freely serve your chief, that is Christ. (Halsall, 2007)

If we read each section individually, we may recognize some of the rhetorical techniques we are trying to teach our students: enconium, epiplexis, pathos, invective, etc. Then, if we study the chiasmus structure, we may see particular points emphasized. Halsall thoroughly discusses the chiasmus in his article but for our purposes, we simply need to recognize that Gregory's preface required no little rhetorical skill. (Halsall, 2007) At the center of Gregory's chiasmus, he tells the kings that their greed for more power indicates their lack of faith in God. Their lack of contentment will be their downfall and the downfall of their people. Halsall puts forth that when all of the prefaces are read together, they teach that the desire for earthly things is the cause of all trouble. Gregory longs for the Merovingian kings to resemble Clovis, who was the "ideal" king and succeeded because he followed God's Word. Critics have complained about Gregory's atrociously poor ability to write in Latin. If one considers the political upheaval of his day and the lack of resources available, we must nonetheless conclude that Gregory is an impressive historian.

## II The Venerable Bede (A.D. 673–735): The History of the English Church and People

Christians around the world sing "A Hymn of Glory Let Us Sing" (Bede, 2006, p. 493) on Ascension Day. This beloved hymn was written by a scholarly monk from Jarrow, Northumbria, who would eventually be known as the "Father of English History." This monk, the "Venerable" Bede, presented his *History of the English Church and People* to King Ceowulf in 731 A.D. It is the history of the metamorphosis of Britain from a land of tribes with opposing interests into a nation with one faith in Jesus Christ. A few short years after he wrote his *History*, Bede passed from this life . . . on Ascension Day.

> *The History of the English Church and People* is one of Bede's last works. He was better known in his day for his numerous commentaries on the books of the Bible and for his textbooks on grammar. He benefited from the excellent library at the monastery of Jarrow. His abbot had traveled as far as Rome to gather books for his library; it is said to have had 300–500 codices.(Bede, 1968, p. 38) Bede's works reflect that he was familiar with at least some of the Latin and Greek Church Fathers: Augustine, Jerome's and Rufinus' translations of Eusebius' *Chronicle*, Ambrose, Gregory I, as well as John Chrysostom and Evagrius' translation of Athanasius. Other important sources were Josephus, Gildas, Orosius, Isidore of Seville, Cassiodorus, Gregory of Tours, and Virgil. (Laistner, 1933)

Bede's work was written in Latin. "It is well to remind oneself, moreover, in order properly to appraise the magnitude of Bede's achievement, that Latin was a foreign language to the people of England. Bede's mastery over Latin idiom, like the German Einhard's a century later, is the more outstanding." (Laistner, 1933) He saw Latin as a uniting factor for the Britons. Bede tells us that the people of Albion spoke British, Pictish, Scottish, and English. They may have come from different tribes "but all are united in their study of God's truth by the fifth (language)—Latin—which has become a common medium through the study of the scriptures." (Bede, 1968) Unity in Christ is the major theme of Bede's *History*.

Bede is not content with an all-inclusive Christianity; he wants to follow the teachings of the Church of Rome, which he believes to be pure doctrine. The arrival of Arianism in Britain is greatly distressing to Bede: "The Christian churches in Britain continued to enjoy this peace until the time of the Arian heresy. This poisonous error after corrupting the whole world, at length crossed the sea and infected even this remote island; and, once the doorway has been opened, every sort of pestilential heresy at once poured into this island, whose people are ready to listen to anything novel, and never hold firm to anything." (Bede, 1968, p. 48) Bede continues in his next chapter with Pelagius: "In his [Arcadius'] time, the Briton Pelagius spread far and wide his noxious and abominable teaching that man had no need of God's grace, and in this he was supported by Julian of Campania. Saint Augustine and other orthodox fathers quoted many Catholic authorities against them, but they refused to abandon their folly. . . ." (Bede, 1968) Bede also discusses the differences of Celtic Christianity with Roman Christianity: the calculation of Easter, the correct wearing of the tonsure, the monastic vs. diocesan rule of the church.

The serious historian may flinch at the miracles Bede includes in his History. Translator Leo Sherley-Price reminds us in his introduction that Bede himself does not claim to have seen the wondrous events; he is merely relaying information from what he considers to be reliable sources (Bede, 1968, p. 31) Sometimes in medieval works, miraculous signs and relics were symbolic of God's approval. (Southern, 1970) Often they were "evidence" of the personal sanctity of the men who performed or witnessed them.

Sherley-Price reminds us: "It is an indication of the temper of the age in which we live that some who profess and call themselves Christians have so little faith in the reality of God's power and mercy that they regard an unmistakable answer to prayer as something unlooked for and extraordinary, almost indecent. It was otherwise among the Christians of Bede's day." (Bede, 1968, p. 31)

What is more interesting than the accounts of healings, holy apparitions, and the like, is a letter written by Pope Gregory I to the missionary Augustine about the miracles he has done. He writes:

> My very dear brother, I hear that Almighty God has worked great wonders through you for the nation which he has chosen. Therefore let your feeling be one of fearful joy at God's heavenly gifts—joy that the souls of the English are being drawn through outward miracles to inward grace; fear lest the frail mind becomes proud because of these wonderful events. . . . For God's chosen do not all work miracles, yet the names of all are written in heaven. For those who are disciples of the truth should rejoice only in that good thing which they share with all men, and which they shall enjoy forever. (Bede, 1968, p. 88)

Miracles are all well and good but such "good works" or examples of piety are not the focus of Christianity; rather, Gregory I wants Christians to be looking forward to their eternal life in heaven. With the backdrop of Christianity Bede's *History* is written for the moral edification of his reader. Here is Bede's introduction:

> For if history records good things of good men, the thoughtful hearer is encouraged to imitate what is good: or if it records evil of wicked men, the devout, religious listener or reader is encouraged to avoid all that is sinful and perverse and to follow what he knows to be good and pleasing to God. Your Majesty is well aware of this; and since you feel so deeply responsible for the general good of those over whom divine Providence has set you, you wish that this history may be made better known both to yourself and to your people. (Bede, 1968, p. 33)

C. S. Lewis and R. W. Southern both explain that the purpose of medieval histories was not to provide a blow-by-blow account of events. Annals did that quite faithfully. Rather, histories were stories. Lewis points out that the word "history" and "story" meant the same thing as late as Queen Elizabeth's time. (Lewis, 2004, p. 179) "It follows that the distinction between history and fiction cannot, in its modern clarity, be applied to medieval books or to the spirit in which they were read." (Lewis, 2004) These stories, whether true or not, were for enjoyment and entertainment. They were also to serve as examples, in Bede's case, usually of piety, to encourage the reader. Furthermore, they were to honor the memory of the great deeds done by great men. (Lewis, 2004, p. 177)

Bede does a couple of things that reassure his readers of the authenticity of his facts. First of all, he takes great pains to list all of his sources, especially noting the expertise of Abbot Albinus, Archbishop Theodore, Abbot Hadrian, and Nothelm.(Bede, 1968, pp.33-35) He begs forgiveness for any inaccuracies and reminds his reader that "as the laws of history require, I have laboured honestly to transmit whatever I could ascertain from common report for the instruction of posterity." (Bede, 1968, p. 35) Secondly, Bede designed a new method of dating historical events. He decided to date everything in relation to the Incarnation of Jesus Christ.[1] Bede obtained this idea from the work of Dionysius Exiguus, whose

---

[1]Note Bede did not date things from the *birth* of Christ but from the *Incarnation*, meaning at conception.

method of calculating the church calendar was accepted at the Synod of Whitby in Britain in A.D. 664. Bede's B.C. and A.D. dating system finally caught on in Europe in the 11th century.

Historian of Late Antiquity, Peter Brown, calls Bede "an evergreen." (Brown, 2007, p. 10) One simply cannot be a serious student of English history without reading his History of the English Church and People.

### III Einhard (A.D. 742–840): Life of Charlemagne

Einhard's *Vita Caroli*, probably written between A.D. 829 and A.D. 836, is a significant history for two reasons. First of all, it is the biography of Charlemagne, the first Holy Roman Emperor, crowned in A.D. 800. Second, Einhard's work is an example of the achievements from Charlemagne's mini-renaissance.

Charlemagne, a Christian Frank, brought much of Germany and France under his own rule. His ability to provide relative peace and stability to the land allowed scholarship some of the leisure time it needed to flourish. He drew scholars such as Alcuin to his court in Aachen. Einhard discusses Charlemagne's interest in learning:

> He paid the greatest attention to the liberal arts; and he had great respect for the men who taught them, bestowing high honors upon them. When he was learning the rules of grammar he received tuition from Peter the Deacon of Pisa, who was by then an old man, but for all other subjects he was taught by Alcuin, surnamed Albinus, another Deacon, a man of the Saxon race who came from Britain and was the most learned man anywhere to be found. Under him the Emperor spent much time and effort in studying rhetoric, dialectic and especially astrology. . . . He also tried to learn to write. With this object in view he used to keep writing-tablets and notebooks under the pillows on his bed, so that he could try his hand at forming letters during his leisure moments; but, although he tried very hard, he had begun too late in life and he made little progress. (Thorpe, 1988, p. 79)

It is easy to snicker at Charlemagne's hoping for some sort of academic osmosis; however, Einhard tells us that Charlemagne could speak Latin and understand Greek. (Thorpe, 1988) Charlemagne also tried to apply his knowledge of grammar to his own language. (Thorpe, 1988, p. 82) Charlemagne never became a proficient reader but he often had works read to him during meals. Augustine's *City of God* was one of Charlemagne's favorites. (Thorpe, 1988, p. 78)

From the time of Cassiodorus in the early 6th century, monasteries had been the repositories for Latin and Greek classics. Monks diligently copied and preserved whatever works they could. Copying the ancient works was difficult because of the style of handwriting, the running together of words, or the lack of understanding on the part of the monks. During the Carolingian Renaissance, some improvements were made. Monks began using lower and upper case letters and putting spaces between the words. As Latin was "restored as a literary language," (Thorpe, 1988, p. 11) corrections were made to some texts. "The debt of literature to the Carolingian copying-schools may be best brought home to us by a very simple consideration. If we set aside Catullus, Tibullus, Propertius and Silius Italicus, together with the tragedies of Seneca and parts of Statius and Claudian, we owe the preservation of practically the whole of Latin poetry to the schools at the time of Charlemagne. These same scholars preserved to us, except for Varro, Tacitus and Apuleius, practically the whole of the prose literature of Rome." (Thorpe, 1988)

Einhard's biography of Charlemagne is one of the products of the Carolingian Renaissance. We now turn to R. W. Southern's expertise for some insights on historians of this age. Southern explains that histories gave medievals an opportunity to apply their rhetorical skills. We recall that rhetoric is the highest level of the trivium but that it appeared to have little practical use in medieval life. The most common histories available at Einhard's time would have given medieval scholars license to see history as literature, and therefore, an art. And, interestingly enough, the Poetics of Aristotle were not recovered until the 13th century, and so the medievals did not know that he would not have approved of their approach to history.

Southern explains Aristotle's position: history is too messy to be an art. It "lacks form because the events of history have no dramatic unity." (Southern, 1970, pp. 175-176) Furthermore, history cannot have balance because events happen without a clear "beginning, middle, and end." This haphazard quality of history is also problematic in that it cannot present one "universal truth." Perhaps the medievals would not have been daunted by Aristotle, as their Christian worldview certainly provided any necessary universal truth and unity.

According to Southern, there were five main authors that would have influenced Einhard: Sallust, Suetonius, Virgil, Lucan, and Boethius. (Southern, 1970, p. 177) The main ideas taken from these histories were:

1) The subject matter of history deserved the exalted language and balance required by rhetoric.

2) Histories provide the "big picture" of what transpired. They are not the place for lists of facts. A little elaboration here and there made the story more interesting.

3) Many authors imitated Virgil's idea of the "destiny of a nation." (Southern, 1970, p. 188) If one could prove that his nation descended from Troy, that would help establish the right of that people to rule over others. How else does one transform murdering marauders into noble leaders?

One final point of interest is Southern's medieval approach to historical causation. Although they had Sallust (86–34 B.C.) as an example, medievals did not imitate his interest in finding a cause for events. For medievals, all was in God's hands. He punished wicked rulers and blessed faithful ones. (Southern, 1970, p. 188) C. S. Lewis agrees with Southern. Medieval man understood the world in terms of "Creation, Fall, Redemption, and Judgement." (Lewis, 2004, p. 174) It is this understanding that gives medieval histories their unity and balance. Furthermore, having seen the fall of the great Roman Empire and living with the remnants of it, the medievals kept very much in mind that this world is fleeting. The allegory of Lady Fortune, well-developed in Boethius's *Consolation of Philosophy*, illustrated how a person could have every earthly good one day and lose it all the next. Better to keep your eyes on eternal things. Such was the medieval view of historical causality.

Einhard is often criticized for borrowing so heavily from Seutonius' (A.D. 75–160) *Lives of the Caesars*. If a reader approaches his *The Life of Charlemagne* as Southern recommends, he will find a rich, elaborate, and enjoyable history.

**IV Dino Compagni (A.D 1260–1324): Chronicle of Florence**

Finally, despite limited information available in English about Compagni; I have chosen to recommend this last lesser-known history primarily because it is so well written and engaging, often fulfilling Southern's artistic requirements of history. Compagni's descriptions of events are realistic, his use of rhetoric is appropriate and effective, and his work is balanced. His reader cannot help but feel grieved by the atrocities committed during the power struggles of Compagni's day.

Dino Compagni was a contemporary of Dante and Giotto in the very turbulent 13th and 14th century Florence. He was a devout Christian silk-merchant who held a variety of public offices through the years. Compagni's love for his city and his love for justice finally moved him to write about the violence he witnessed. Unlike the previously discussed historians, Compagni was neither a monk nor a court scholar, but he was obviously educated. Florence at this time was wealthy enough for a good number of its population of 100,000 to attend school. Compagni's fellow historian, Giovanni Villani, wrote that about 10,000 boys and girls were learning to read and write in his day. (Compagni, 1986, p. 5) It is interesting to note that Compagni, like Dante, wrote his work in the vernacular.

Compagni's *Chronicle* brilliantly tells of the clashes of the Guelfs and the Ghibellines, beginning with the murder of Buondelmonte de Buondelmonti in 1215 and finishing in 1312. If the reader is unfamiliar with the history of Florence, all of the names of the various factions may be overwhelming; just read the work and analyze it later. Eventually Chapters 21 and 22 in Book II make everything clear. Finally, toward the end of the history, in 1309, Compagni has great hope for peace because Henry, count of Luxembourg, was annointed Holy Roman Emperor. There had been no Holy Roman Emperor for nearly 60 years! Compagni's work ends in 1312 with Henry about to set upon Florence. Unfortunately, Henry withdrew and died a year later, leaving Compagni out of political favor and his work unknown for about 300 years. (Compagni, 1986, p. xxvii)

**Conclusion**

C. S. Lewis's character Eustace from *The Voyage of The Dawn Treader* is a great caricature of our modern society's fascination with facts and science. While Lucy and Edmond knew the reality of dragons, Eustace "liked books if they were books of information and had pictures of grain elevators or of fat foreign children doing exercises in model schools." (Lewis, 1952, p. 2) We are much too clever to believe in fairy tales or "untrustworthy monkish flapdoodle."

In Peter Brown's speech at the opening of the Oxford Centre for Late Antiquity, he reminded his audience of a time when historians only looked at public records and annals of the medievals because they wanted the cold hard facts. Histories and chronicles "were the work of monkish chroniclers, whose tendency to exaggeration, whose moral bias and whose pervasive Catholic ideology made them as distasteful as they were unreliable." The refusal to read the works created "a Philistinism which had to be heard to be believed. And hear it I did. I heard a leading College Fellow in medieval history announce, with relief, that: 'Now that we have got rid of Dante, I can get down to Henry III and the Barons.'" Brown recalls that it was R. W. Southern who took the lead in teaching scholars that "literary texts awash with cultural meaning might serve as guides to the past quite as much as did the archives of the Public Record Office. . . ." (Brown, 2007)

History's red-headed step-child will never turn into Cinderella. Lady Fortune will not provide her with a Prince Charming. Rather, she will wear the hair shirt and remember that there once was a better time, and she will hope for the future.

---

Angela Hill, B.A. History from Indiana University, wife to the Reverend John Hill, is a classical Lutheran homeschooler, classroom teacher, and frequent speaker at conferences of the Consortium for Classical and Lutheran Education.

# Cassiodorus and Luther: Historical Foundations for Classical Lutheran Education

*by Rev. John E. Hill*

The rebirth of the classical philosophy of education in the Lutheran Church - Missouri Synod has not yet met with as much enthusiastic acclaim by its teachers, schools, and parents as one might expect. Indeed, in some places this philosophy has become foreign to the confessional church where it was once at home. Those who have rediscovered this ancient understanding of education are faced with the daunting task of rebuilding on a foundation that is difficult to uncover. For Lutherans, the Christian school has historically been a matter of congregational necessity, as can be seen in Luther's *Instructions for the Visitors of Parish Pastors* (1528) and the original Constitution of the Lutheran Church - Missouri Synod (1847); in both cases, an education based upon classical forms was the norm.

Clearly a transition has taken place among confessional Lutherans. Educators may well explore the inroads of Rationalism, Romanticism, and Modernism into the academic education establishment and ask the extent to which the contemporary philosophies and scientific theories of man and his world accurately reflect the doctrine of Scriptures and the Lutheran Confessions. They may further examine the extent to which these philosophies and theories inform the suppositions and methodologies of those who strive to be worthy of the title 'Lutheran Teacher.' For those who recognize the failures and deceptions of modern progressive education, another transition is required. Much work is needed to counter the assumptions of a progressive philosophy that is currently in the firm grip of Freudian psychology, Darwinian theory, and postmodern social constructs. Much has been accepted uncritically from the 20th and 21st century education establishment.

Classical Lutheran schools need to rediscover the historical basis upon which they are founded. Where did Christian schools begin, and why? What was their purpose? What was the role of the Christian school in those critical moments in Church history, such as the Reformation? What theological considerations and pedagogical goals were most important in forming their curriculum? Classical Roman Catholics turn to Thomas Aquinas and Augustine for answers. Calvinists build on the writings of John Calvin and also of Augustine. Lutherans certainly look to Martin Luther, Philip Melanchthon, and the Lutheran Confessions for the theological foundation for their schools.

This paper does not presume to answer all these questions, but rather attempts the more modest goal of comparing two figures in our ecclesiastical history who proposed an educational program for their day that parallels our own efforts. Our goal here is to begin exploring the historical underpinnings of a classical Christian education. This article looks at the reflections of churchmen who advocated beginning, or beginning anew, broadly Christian and classical schools.

## Cassiodorus

Our examination begins with a scholar who might be described as belonging to the second generation of the transition into the classical enculturation of Christianity during the fifth and sixth centuries of the Christian era. St. Jerome and St. Augustine led the first generation. The contribution of Jerome to his academic world included especially his translation of Scripture into Latin and the compilation of a bibliography of Christian authors. Augustine is especially remembered in the history of Western culture for his *Confessions* and *City of God*, and for bringing secular and Scriptural teaching together in his fourth book of *On Christian Doctrine*.

Boethius, best known for his *Consolation of Philosophy*, belongs to the second generation of this transition, as does Cassiodorus, his younger contemporary. Although Cassiodorus clearly built on the work of these first three Church fathers, he was the first to propose a single program for divine and secular education. David Wagner asserts, "Cassiodorus's advocacy of the liberal arts as a necessary component of Christian education was decisive for the assimilation of the liberal arts within Christian culture." (Wagner, 1983, p. 20) This assimilation of the liberal arts into a newly forming Christian culture laid the foundation for classical Christian schools.

Born around 490 in Scyllaceum in southern Italy along the coast of the Ionian Sea, Cassiodurus conducted a brilliant career. As a statesman, he served in succession as councilor to his father, the governor of Sicily, quaestor, consul, magister officiorum (succeeding the condemned Boethius), and finally as praetorian prefect for all of Italy, effectively the prime minister of the Ostrogothic civil government. Cassiodorus was a survivor of the scholar-bureaucrat in the early 6th century barbarian court of Theodoric the Ostrogoth and his successors. After his retirement in 537/8 he traveled to Constantinople, there gaining knowledge of Byzantine theology and the Greek language and culture. He returned to Italy in 554, gathering to himself at his family estate a monastic community (named *Vivarium*) committed to the preservation and transmission of both sacred and secular books. He died about 585.

Cassiodorus was born into the transition in which the knowledge and education of the ancient world was passing from the aristocratic and senatorial classes to the bishops and monasteries. With the breakdown of Roman culture under the barbarians, local communities were led primarily by their religious leaders, who became the new academic elite, though without the cultivated leisure of the ancient world. Cassiodorus lived in the brief window between the earlier hostile relations of secular culture and Christianity, on the one hand, and the descent of barbarian darkness, on the other. In this rapidly closing window, Cassiodorus was able to engage in the leisure that had marked ancient scholarship, but as a Christian, reading, copying, writing, and collecting his famous library at the *Vivarium*. This is the context in which he proposed the formation of the first Christian school.

In his day, all education for lay Christians was given in two entirely separate venues. One was the Baptismal catechesis and liturgy of the Church. This catechesis is well documented under Augustine and others in the Fourth and Fifth Centuries. The other institutions for education were the surviving ancient secular schools of grammar and rhetoric which still flourished in Rome for the well-to-do. The only alternative to catechesis for the study of Scripture was to enter a monastic community like the monastery and library Cassiodorus founded in southern Italy in his very long retirement. The idea of a Christian "school" that teaches both divine and secular learning was unknown and had not previously been suggested or attempted.

Writing after his return to Italy in 1554, Cassiodorus began his school proposal with this introduction:

> When I realized that there was such a zealous and eager pursuit of secular learning, by which the majority of mankind hopes to obtain knowledge of this world, I was deeply grieved, I admit, that Holy Scripture should so lack public teachers, whereas secular authors certainly flourish in widespread teaching. Together with blessed Pope Agapetus of Rome, I made efforts to collect money so that it should rather be the Christian schools in the city of Rome that could employ learned teachers – the money having been collected – from whom the faithful might gain eternal salvation for their souls and the adornment of sober and pure eloquence for their speech. (Cassiodorus et al., 2004, p. 20)

The Christian school that Cassiodorus envisioned did not come into being. "I could not accomplish this task because of raging wars and violent struggles in the Kingdom of Italy – for a peaceful endeavour has no place in a time of unrest". (Cassiodorus et al., 2004) Rome was brought under the sway of Constantinople during the years 535-540 by Justinian's general, Belisarius, who entered Ravenna in 540. Agapetus, who was pope from 535-536, died in Constantinople while protesting Justinian's policy. Cassiodorus himself was probably taken to Constantinople and remained there from 540-554.

In the broader picture of their historical circumstances, Cassiodorus and Agapetus had recognized the need for Christian schools because, in those chaotic times, the knowledge and teaching of Holy Scripture was in danger of being lost to men unskilled in either the Greek or Latin languages in which it was found. Furthermore, they saw that an apologetic was needed to appeal to the educated aristocratic and senatorial class, from whom, in the years to come, the bishops of the church were chosen and who exerted leadership in the dark centuries that followed. Finally, the theological chaos of those years required that the church of the Chalcedonian Confession be given the tools and training to defend itself against the doctrinal pressures of Eutychianism, Nestorianism, and Monophysitism from the East, and from the Arianism of their Ostrogothic overlords in Italy.

In other words, the combination of the loss of Rome's political power to both the barbarians and the East, and the incursions of heretical doctrine from all sides, awakened the need for a specifically Christian education to keep Rome as the beacon of catholic Christianity. The Holy Scriptures themselves demanded an educated Church that could rightly handle the text and doctrine of the Bible, and simultaneously provide leaders for government and civil service in a Christian land.

Cassiodorus wrote the *Institutions of Divine and Secular Learning* to fill this need. This is where classical Christian education's traditional appeal to St Augustine is somewhat inadequate. Augustine's treatise, "On Christian Doctrine," is directed to cultivating the wisdom and eloquence of the teachers of Christian doctrine in his day, that is, pastors. The fourth book of this treatise, written in 426, is a manual for Christian preaching. As a whole, the work assumes that schools *outside the church* would provide classically trained recruits for the clergy; these school were not Christian, nor were they taught by Christians. Augustine did not change this paradigm and was reluctant to integrate fully the classical tradition into his seminary instruction, even avoiding the terms of the trivium, grammar, dialectic, and rhetoric. Nevertheless, Cassiodorus appealed to Augustine as his most influential Latin Father, who, along with Jerome, had begun to recognize and speak of a distinction between divine and secular learning, or literature. Jerome and Augustine had prepared the way for the Christian commendation of the pagan classical tradition. Augustine's "On Christian Doctrine" provided the bridge between this ancient classical tradition and Christianity, and was viewed throughout the Middle Ages as the beginning of a uniquely Christian culture.

Cassiodorus was the first to make use of this bridge between pagan classicism and the Christian Scriptures when he proposed the curriculum for a Christian school. He brought together the bibliographical work of Jerome and the surviving literature of the classical tradition. Writing more than a century after Augustine, Cassiodorus showed no hesitation in synthesizing the liberal arts tradition with the teaching of God's Word. The title of his treatise summarized its content, "Institutions of Divine and Secular Learning." Peter Brown, in *Rise of Western Christendom*, writes:

> In Cassiodorus' view, all Latin literature was to be mobilized towards transmitting the Scrip-
> tures. All the aids previously used so as to read and copy classical texts were to be used

to understand the Scriptures and to copy them intelligently. Like a newly formed planetary system, Latin culture as a whole was supposed to spin in orbit around the vast sun of the Word of God.

In order to make a better comparison between Cassiodorus and Luther, we turn briefly to the curriculum proposed in the "Institutions of Divine and Secular Learning." His description of the curriculum is also the sketch of its underpinnings and assumptions. Singularly unoriginal in being based on established canonical Scriptures, accepted Church Fathers, and the widely recognized literature of the seven liberal arts, it is unique and important for proposing the integration of these two areas of learning so simply and plainly in the changing world of the mid sixth century.

> I was moved by divine love to devise for you, with God's help, these introductory books to take the place of a teacher. Through them I believe that both the textual sequence of Holy Scripture and also a compact account of secular letters may, with God's grace, be revealed. . . . They are of great use as an introduction to the source both of the knowledge of this world and of the salvation of the soul. (Cassiodorus et al., 2004, p. 105)

Cassiodorus continued, "So in the first book you have teachers of a former age always available and prepared to teach you." (Cassiodorus et al., 2004, p. 107) The first book, on divine learning, summarized the Scriptures of the Old and New Testaments, the Apocrypha (Hagiographa), and the four Ecumenical Councils. With each of these writings Cassiodorus recommended and summarized specific commentaries and sermons written by the earlier fathers, the likes of Augustine, Ambrose, Jerome, Basil, Prosper, Origen, and Athanasius, including also newly commissioned or newly translated works. Then he recommended the Christian histories and the geographies, and closed the first book with advice to monastic congregations, such as his own, into whose charge he gave the copying of texts.

The second book of the "Institutions" is organized into seven sections for each of the liberal arts: the three arts of the trivium (grammar, rhetoric, and dialectic); and the four disciplines of mathematics (arithmetic, music, geometry, and astronomy). For each Cassiodorus gave a summary of its content and again suggested the works of recognized authors for instruction. "The obvious purpose," he writes of this order of the secular disciplines, "was to direct our mind, which has been dedicated to secular wisdom and cleansed by the exercise of the disciplines, from earthly things and to place it in a praiseworthy fashion in the divine structure." (Cassiodorus et al., 2004, p. 229) In his conclusion, Cassiodorus set secular and divine learning into their own fitting place, "because," he wrote, "from time to time we gain from secular letters commendable knowledge of some matters, but from divine law we gain eternal life." (Cassiodorus et al., 2004, p. 230) He finally commended the student to a contemplation of the Apocalypse of St John, to meditation of the Holy Trinity, and to anticipation of the beatific vision.

## Luther

Dr. Martin Luther proposed the reformation of the Christian school in a context that was in many ways similar to that of Cassiodorus, though 1000 years later. Secular learning, preserved almost exclusively by bishops and monks through most of that time period, had begun to return to secular institutions in the late Middle Ages and early Renaissance. The knowledge and authority of Scriptures, however, had become obscured and supplanted by the theology and institutions of the Roman papacy. The Turkish threat, the Peasants' revolt, and the nascent struggles between Roman and Evangelical forces, all were reminiscent of the chaos and transition of Cassiodorus' day.

But was there a connection between Cassiodorus and Luther? Luther was certainly familiar with Cassiodorus' "Explanation of the Psalms" and used this work favorably and extensively in his first lectures on the Psalms. Cassiodorus' commentary on the Psalms, which Luther digested thoroughly at the beginning of his career as a lecturer in 1513-1515, is an argument for the use of the clasical tradition, and the work is echoed in Luther's school treatises of the 1520s. For example, Cassiodorus wrote in the "Explanation",

> Those experienced in the secular arts, clearly living long after the time when the first words of the divine books were penned, transferred these techniques to the collections of arguments which the Greeks called topics, and to the arts of dialectic and rhetoric. So it is crystal clear to all that the minds of the just were endowed to express the truth with the techniques which pagans subsequently decided should be exploited for human wisdom. In the sacred readings (*lectionibus sacris*) they shine like the brightest of stars, aptly clarifying the meanings of passages most usefully and profitably. (Cassiodorus and Walsh, 1990, pp. 37-38)

Again, in his exposition of Psalm 150, Cassiodorus showed even further how he made the Psalter a textbook in the liberal arts. "We have shown that the series of psalms is crammed with points of grammar, etymologies, figures, rhetoric, topics, dialectic, definitions, music, geometry [and] astronomy", (Cassiodorus and Walsh, 1990, p. 150) in other words, all seven liberal arts.

While the present writer did not find direct evidence that Luther had read Cassiodorus' "Institutions of Divine and Secular Learning," his own program of schooling closely parallels that of Cassiodorus. See Luther's treatise of 1520, "To the Christian Nobility", where he wrote early in the Reformation:

> Above all, the foremost reading for everybody, both in the universities and in the schools, should be Holy Scripture and for the younger boys, the Gospels. And would to God that every town had a girls' school as well, where the girls would be taught the gospel for an hour every day either in German or in Latin. . . Is it not right that every Christian man know the entire holy gospel by the age of nine or ten? Does he not derive his name and his life from the gospel? . . . I would advise no one to send his child where the Holy Scriptures are not supreme. Every institution that does not unceasingly pursue the study of God's word becomes corrupt. . . I greatly fear that the universities, unless they teach the Holy Scriptures diligently and impress them on the young students, are wide gates to hell. (Luther, 1995, vol. 44, pp. 205-207)

Luther's words articulate the same goal as Cassiodorus for creating Christian schools with Scripture as their center. There is, however, also a hint of Augustine's caution over secular learning. Luther was reluctant to allow human reason too great of an opportunity to supplant Holy Scriptures.

Four years later, when Luther addressed more directly the need for Christian schools, he did not show the same hesitation about secular learning. He embraced the liberal arts of the classical tradition and urged their use. He wrote in 1524, "To the Councilmen of All Cities in Germany that they Establish and Maintain Christian Schools":

A city's best and greatest welfare, safety, and strength consist rather in its having many able, learned, wise, honorable, and well-educated citizens. They can then readily gather, protect, and properly use treasure and all manner of property.

So it was done in ancient Rome. There boys were so taught that by the time they reached their fifteenth, eighteenth, or twentieth year they were well versed in Latin, Greek, and all the liberal arts (as they are called), and then immediately entered upon a political or military career. Their system produced intelligent, wise, and competent men, so skilled in every art and rich in experience that if all the bishops, priests, and monks in the whole of Germany today were rolled into one, you would not have the equal of a single Roman soldier. As a result their country prospered; they had capable and trained men for every position. So at all times throughout the world simple necessity has forced men, even among the heathen, to maintain pedagogues and schoolmasters if their nation was to be brought to a high standard. Hence, the word "schoolmaster" is used by Paul in Galatians 4 as a word taken from the common usage and practice of mankind, where he says, "The law was our schoolmaster." (Luther, 1995, vol. 45, pp. 356-359)

Luther revealed here not only his own reading of the ancient classics, but he recognized their continued usefulness for producing citizens that could fill every need. A Christian city or country needed more than Holy Scriptures; it also needed the best education the world could give. Luther was urging the joining of divine and secular learning in the schools of the Reformation.

But the heart of a good education, Luther proposed, was the written and spoken word. Both "kingdoms" are ruled and defended by means of language. So Luther continued:

"All right," you say again, "suppose we do have to have schools; what is the use of teaching Latin, Greek, and Hebrew, and the other liberal arts? We could just as well use German for teaching the Bible and God's word, which is enough for our salvation." I reply: Alas! I am only too well aware that we Germans must always be and remain brutes and stupid beasts . . . . Languages and the arts, which can do us no harm, but are actually a greater ornament, profit, glory, and benefit, both for the understanding of Holy Scripture and the conduct of temporal government–these we despise. . . .

Truly, if there were no other benefit connected with the languages, this should be enough to delight and inspire us, namely, that they are so fine and noble a gift of God, with which he is now so richly visiting and blessing us Germans above all other lands. We do not see many instances where the devil has allowed them to flourish . . . . For the devil smelled a rat, and perceived that if the languages were revived a hole would be knocked in his kingdom which he could not easily stop up again. . .

Although the gospel came and still comes to us through the Holy Spirit alone, we cannot deny that it came through the medium of languages, was spread abroad by that means, and must be preserved by the same means. . . . In proportion then as we value the gospel, let us zealously hold to the languages. (Luther, 1995, vol. 45, pp. 356-359)

Luther reflected here the same conviction that drove the Grammarians of the early Middle Ages to teach and emphasize Grammar. Latin had ceased to be the common language, Greek was almost unknown in the West, and the Word of God and all the written treasures of the Ancient Church and of the Ancient World were on the verge of being lost. The preservation and use of the Word of God was for Luther, as it had been for Cassiodorus, the first and central purpose for all schooling among Christians. Luther took this position because of the conviction that faith and Church are established and preserved, defended and spread abroad only through the Word of God. As far as Luther was concerned, all the future of the Church's doctrine was bound up in the schools. Just as Cassiodorus recognized the need for Christian schools in his conflicted times, so Luther saw the same need in the struggles of the Reformation.

Luther's second, urgent purpose for Christian schools turned from the spiritual estate to the temporal estate or government. He continued in *To the Councilmen*:

> It is not necessary to repeat here that the temporal government is a divinely ordained estate . . . . The question is rather: How are we to get good and capable men into it? Here we are excelled and put to shame by the pagans of old, especially the Romans and Greeks. Although they had no idea of whether this estate were pleasing to God or not, they were so earnest and diligent in educating and training their young boys and girls to fit them for the task, that when I call it to mind I am forced to blush for us Christians, and especially for us Germans. Yet we know, or at least we ought to know, how essential and beneficial it is–and pleasing to God–that a prince, lord, councilman, or other person in a position of authority be educated and qualified to perform the functions of his office as a Christian should.

> Now if (as we have assumed) there were no souls, and there were no need at all of schools and languages for the sake of the Scriptures and of God, this one consideration alone would be sufficient to justify the establishment everywhere of the very best schools for both boys and girls, namely, that in order to maintain its temporal estate outwardly the world must have good and capable men and women, men able to rule well over land and people, women able to manage the household and train children and servants aright. Now such men must come from our boys, and such women from our girls. Therefore, it is a matter of properly educating and training our boys and girls to that end. . . . (Luther, 1995, vol. 45, pp. 367-368)

You may observe that Luther's temporal estate also included fulfillment of the Christian's vocation. Luther's doctrine of vocation emerged from Scripture in the recognition that the monasticism of his day was no true vocation, because it had neither the command nor the promise of God in His Word. It had become something different from the scriptorium and repository of divine and secular literature of Cassiodorus' monastic community. But all true godly vocations have both the command and promise of God and require able and knowledgeable men and women. Therefore boys and girls need to receive Christian schooling for the maintenance of home, government, and workplace, as well as the church.

Thus Luther developed the two-fold schooling of Cassiodorus, the divine and the secular, into an expression also of the school's purpose. The Christian school serves both the eternal estate in the preservation and teaching of God's Word, and the temporal estate, in the education of the Christian for a life of vocation in this world.

This education is what we call today a classical, Lutheran education. In his 1524 treatise, Luther integrated the ancient classical curriculum with the teaching of God's Word, just as Cassiodorus had done a thousand years earlier. We read,

> But if children were instructed and trained in schools, or wherever learned and well-trained schoolmasters and schoolmistresses were available to teach the languages, the other arts, and history, they would then hear of the doings and sayings of the entire world, and how things went with various cities, kingdoms, princes, men, and women. Thus, they could in a short time set before themselves as in a mirror the character, life, counsels, and purposes–successful and unsuccessful–of the whole world from the beginning; on the basis of which they could then draw the proper inferences and in the fear of God take their own place in the stream of human events. In addition, they could gain from history the knowledge and understanding of what to seek and what to avoid in this outward life, and be able to advise and direct others accordingly. . . .

> For my part, if I had children and could manage it, I would have them study not only languages and history, but also singing and music together with the whole of mathematics [i.e. the quadrivium: arithmetic, music, geometry, astronomy]. For what is all this but mere child's play? The ancient Greeks trained their children in these disciplines; yet they grew up to be people of wondrous ability, subsequently fit for everything. How I regret now that I did not read more poets and historians, and that no one taught me them! (Luther, 1995, vol. 45, pp. 268-369)

Luther even adds a sort of curriculum book list, just as Cassiodorus had done, as a suggested source for the program of education he envisions:

> First of all, there would be the Holy Scriptures, in Latin, Greek, Hebrew, and German, and any other language in which they might be found. Next, the best commentaries, and, if I could find them, the most ancient, in Greek, Hebrew, and Latin. Then, books that would be helpful in learning the languages, such as the poets and orators, regardless of whether they were pagan or Christian, Greek or Latin, for it is from such books that one must learn grammar. After that would come books on the liberal arts, and all the other arts. Finally, there would be books of law and medicine; there too there should be careful choices among commentaries.

> Among the foremost would be the chronicles and histories, in whatever languages they are to be had. For they are a wonderful help in understanding and guiding the course of events, and especially for observing the marvelous works of God. (Luther, 1995, vol. 45, p. 376) . . .

More citations can be adduced from Luther. Four years later, in his *Instructions for the Visitors of Parish Pastors* (Luther, 1995, vol. 40) Luther gave direction to the ecclesiastical visitors concerning their oversight not only of churches, but also the churches' schools. "The preachers are to exhort the people to send their children to school so that persons are educated for competent service both in church and state". (Luther, 1995, vol. 40, p. 314) He gave instructions and laid out a curriculum for three groups, beginning with those who are learning to read and concluding with those who read the Latin of Virgil and speak it in the classroom. Although the focus at this parish level is on Grammar, the third group is directed to study dialectic and rhetoric also.

Two years later, during the summer of the Diet at Augsburg in 1530, Luther wrote "A Sermon on Keeping Children in School". (Luther, 1995, vol. 46) He divided his exhortation into two parts, the first in support of the church and the teaching of future pastors, and second in support of the temporal estate, supporting especially the government, but also other vocations. "Where are the preachers, jurists, and physicians to come from, if grammar and other rhetorical arts are not taught. For such teaching is the spring from which they all must flow". (Luther, 1995, vol. 46, p. 252) Luther himself sent his son John to such a school in Torgau, as his letter to the headmaster of the Torgau Latin School, testifies. (Luther, 1995, vol. 50, p. 230ff)

## Conclusion

What have we learned from Cassiodorus and Luther? A classical Christian school employs both divine and secular learning. Each of these two areas of instruction serves both the spiritual and the temporal estate, ultimately so that God's Word may be kept and fulfilled in every area of our lives. By teaching God's Word and doctrine, languages, liturgy, church history, and the like, the school prepares some students for service in the Church, and instructs all students for the promotion and defense of the pure Gospel. The school provides training for vocation and produces men and women who are both spiritually and bodily prepared for appropriate service in government, home, church, workplace, and school. This education focuses upon the languages, employs the ancient trivium and quadrivium in its curriculum, and uses history and literature as the core resources of its secular curriculum.

Reflections on Cassiodorus and Luther draw us to examine the challenges which faced these fathers in the Church. The problems of our day are certainly nothing new. Cassiodorus proposed a truly classical and Christian education precisely because this was the education that was most needed for Church and state, and which was unavailable to the 6th century Church. Luther's proposal for a Christian school is almost identical to that of Cassiodorus. The needs were the same, the educational philosophy and curriculum were the same, and the teaching materials were essentially the same. In our day we still have the same needs that must be met with the same schools.

Luther's 1530 sermon on keeping children in school rings true with the particular challenge which confessional Lutherans face in the 21st century. Lutheran parents, congregations, and pastors are still reluctant to expend their resources in giving their children the specifically Lutheran and classical education that the Church has needed and demanded for almost 1500 years. It is our task to urge and exhort the Church of our day to prepare young people not for the earning of money, but for the service of God in vocations in both the church and the temporal estate.

---

The Reverend John Hill is pastor and headmaster of CCLE-accredited Mount Hope Lutheran School in Casper, Wyoming. Writer and speaker for CCLE, he previously served as Board member of the Consortium for Classical and Lutheran Education.

Notes

## Classical Elements in the United States Constitution

*by Dr. E. Christian Kopff*

In the *LA TIMES* for September 24, 2004, two months before the Presidential election of that year, Edward L. Glaeser, Professor of Economics at Harvard, tried to explain what he saw as a paradox. No matter who wins the election in November, Glaeser wrote, "the United States will be the most conservative developed nation in the world. Its economy will remain the least regulated, its welfare state the smallest, its military the strongest and its citizens the most religious." After citing evidence for these assertions, he continued, "It wasn't always so. At the start of the 20th century, the U.S. looked progressive compared with Europe's empires. The big difference between the U.S. and Europe is that the U.S. kept its 18th century Constitution, while most European countries discarded theirs."

No one - not even Professor Glaeser, as his article goes on to show - would attribute all of America's current condition to its Constitution, but few would deny that the Constitution is an important element in what makes America what it is. Glaeser's words provide us with an appropriate text on which to meditate in a publication devoted to classical education. I think he ignored two important considerations. Much of what makes our Constitution distinctive does not come from the 18th century, but from the ancient world. These factors, including the ideas of a mixed constitution and checks and balances, are not two hundred years old, but more than two thousand years old. Secondly, the Founders were well aware of this situation. They were not stuck with political ideas and ideals that were millennia old because nothing more recent was available. On the contrary, they considered their antiquity a mark of their quality and validity.

Scholars defend the essentially Enlightenment character of the Founding by pointing out that many state constitutions explicitly mention the doctrine of balance and separation of powers that was theorized in the 18th century by Montesquieu in his influential *Spirit of the Laws* (1748). The US Constitution, however, institutes what we now call a system of "checks and balances," defended by James Madison in Federalist 47. As historian Jack Rakove explains, the Constitution "sought to preserve the balance and equilibrium of the departments of government not by separating them rigidly, but rather by giving each institution peculiar means of self-defense and by varying the modes of their appointment and their tenure in office." Rakove is correct here, but not when he goes on to write, "In this revised form, separation of powers came to replace the older theory of 'mixed government.'" (Hamilton et al., 2003, p. 117) The Framers of the Constitution were not modifying a modern theory, but returning to the historical models of checks and balances of the Roman republic, as recorded by Livy and theorized by Polybius and Cicero.

When the convention called in 1787 to revise the Articles of Confederation decided to ignore its charge and write a new constitution, the delegates began by debating the structure of the legislature. Should it be unicameral, as delegate Benjamin Franklin hoped and the Enlightenment philosopher Turgot had argued in print, or bicameral, like the influential constitution of Massachusetts, whose author, John Adams, was American ambassador to the Court of St. James in distant London? Adams wrote the first volume of his *Defense of the Constitutions of Government of the United States* to defend the bicameralism of the state constitutions against Turgot and Franklin. He devoted many pages to Polybius VI, the locus classicus for the role of checks and balances in Rome's constitution. Published in January 1787, the first volume crossed the Atlantic by March and was re-printed several times before the Convention opened on May 25. As Gilbert Chinard saw, "Even a casual glance at the records of the Federal Convention will show that Adams' book was used as a sort of repertory by many speakers, who found in it a confirmation of their views, and chiefly convenient illustrations and precedents." (Chinard, 1933, p. 212)

The situation was not lost on Benjamin Franklin, who saw his dreams of a highly centralized government and unicameral legislature disappearing before Adams's arguments and the prestige of the classical tradition. Before the first week was over, on Thursday, May 31, according to Madison's notes, "The 3rd. Resolution, 'that the national legislature ought to consist of two branches,' was agreed to without debate or dissent, except that of Pennsylvania, given probably from complaisance to Doctor Franklin who was understood to be partial to a single House of Legislation." (Farrand, 1987, p. 48)

The month of June went by, filled with classical citations. At last, on June 28, Franklin had had enough. Most of that day and the day before had been spent listening to Luther Martin of Maryland, who defended with frequent references to the ancient world the view that while representation in the House should be based on a state's population, every state should have an equal number of Senators. Madison, who had stopped his usual assiduous note-taking in disgust at the length and content of Martin's speech, rose to object: "There has been much fallacy in the arguments advanced by the gentleman from Maryland." Heated squabbling ensued and finally Franklin rose to speak. We know what he said because he gave a copy of his remarks, which were far from extemporaneous, to Madison to insert into his record of the proceedings of the convention.

> We indeed seem to feel our own want of political wisdom, since we have been running about in search of it. We have gone back to ancient history for models of Government, and examined the different forms of those Republics which having been formed with the seeds of their own dissolution now no longer exist. And we have viewed Modern States all round Europe, but find none of their Constitutions suitable to our circumstances. In this situation of this Assembly, groping as it were in the dark to find political truth, and scarce able to distinguish it when presented to us, how has it happened, Sir, that we have not hitherto once thought of humbly applying to the Father of lights to illuminate our understandings? (Farrand, 1987, pp. 451-452)

After more pious reflections Franklin moved that the local clergy be invited to begin each day's deliberations with prayer. He was asking the delegates to ignore the lessons of history and especially of classical antiquity and trust to their own lucubrations to create the new constitution. For Franklin the Father of Lights had a different and better lesson to teach than the Author of History, with whom He is sometimes confused. Hamilton and several others tried to squelch the resolution. "After several unsuccessful attempts for silently postponing the matter by adjourning," wrote Madison, "the adjournment was at length carried, without any vote on the motion." (Farrand, 1987, pp. 453-458)

The power of the classical tradition over the Framers was so great that they denied the courtesy of a vote to a motion from the Convention's most distinguished member, Benjamin Franklin. This, however, is not the whole story. Although Madison's notes are usually the fullest, in this case, his disgust with Luther Martin led him to ignore an important point, preserved in the laconic jotting of William Patterson of New Jersey: "Amphictyonic Council of Greece represented by two from each town—who were notwithstanding the disproportions of the towns equal — Rollins Ancient History 4 vol. pa.79." (Farrand, 1987, p. 459) "Who would have thought," Gilbert Chinard wrote, "unless such positive texts were produced, that the limitation of two senators for each state might perhaps be traced to the Amphictyonic Council of

Greece." (Chinard, 1940, pp. 38-58) Rather, I would say, who can deny that the documentary record proves that the Amphictyonic League provided the precedent for the idea of two senators from each state? Who can fail to be impressed that this happened in the face of the vigorous objections of James Madison and the weary protests of Benjamin Franklin? Such was the hold that the classical tradition had on the minds of the Framers.

Classical political thought provided the ideas and patterns used by the Framers in their deliberations—for example, that government is best understood as the rule of the one, the few, and the many; and the best government is a mixture of all three. Many since Turgot and Franklin have argued that Americans should ignore this view of government, which is based on ancient Greek and Latin practice and reflection, but, so far, in vain.

John Adams wrote his old friend, Dr. Benjamin Rush on June 19, 1789, "I should as soon think of closing all my window shutters to enable me to see as of banishing the Classicks to improve Republican ideas." (Rush and Butterfield, 1951, p. 518 n. 2) The Framers of the Constitution agreed. They knew that citizenship was a legacy from the ancient world, and free government was safest when founded on a mixed constitution guarded by a system of checks and balances. The traditions they knew and valued are still available in today's world. First, however, we have to keep our window shutters to this classical legacy. That is the mission of educators, parents, and students who are committed to classical education.

----

Dr. E. Christian Kopff, author of *The Devil Knows Latin: Why America Needs the Classical Tradition*, serves as associate professor of classics in the Honors program at the University of Colorado – Boulder.

Notes

## How Classical Christian Education Created the Modern World

*by Dr. E. Christian Kopff*

In 1960 Irving Kristol wrote in the English review *Encounter*, "Future historians may yet decide that one of the crucial events of our century, perhaps decisive for its cultural and political destiny, was the gradual dissolution and abandonment of the study of the classics as the core of the school curriculum." (Kristol, 2011, p. 111) Just as the abandonment of studying the classics and the classical curriculum that accompanied and explained them was "crucial and perhaps decisive" for the Twentieth Century, so the spread of the classical curriculum from the education of clergy and clerks at cathedral schools and cloisters in the Middle Ages to aristocratic courts in the Renaissance and then to schools for subjects and citizens in the Reformation and its aftermath was decisive for religious revival, scientific discovery and political freedom in the Modern Era.

Despite curricular differences in various parts of Europe, classical Christian education in early modern Europe shared certain fundamental traits. There was a balance between instruction in the arts of language and the arts of mathematics, the trivium and quadrivium. The arts of language were taught as (Latin) grammar, dialectic (or logic) and rhetoric. The reading lists of the curriculum were taken from what German classicist Manfred Fuhrmann calls the Two Canons, the Bible and the pagan classics.(Fuhrmann, 2002, pp. 9-13) This curriculum educated the people who created the Modern World.

The idea that Martin Luther was hostile to the pagan classics is found in the twentieth century from committed classical Christian educators like Louis Markos to learned specialists like Harvard's Douglas Bush. The origins of this error may be due to the background radiation from Luther's polemic with Erasmus, who had a tendency to treat his opponents as enemies of "good letters." It would be an unacceptable simplification to treat the Reformation as primarily the result of educational reform, but it is equally unacceptable to ignore the role of classical Christian education in the creative turmoil of the sixteenth century. In his letter to Humanist poet Eobanus Hessus 1523, Luther insisted that his theology was compatible with Humanist ideals. "Without knowledge of literature, pure theology cannot exist, as until now, with letters collapsing in ruins, theology fell most pitifully and lay ruined. I see there has never been a great revelation of God's Word unless He first prepared the way by the rise and flourishing of languages and letters." (WA Br 3: 50; AE 49: 34)

Martin Luther devoted much of his early years at Wittenberg to reforming the university in a humanist mold. Hiring Philip Melanchthon was part of that initiative. (Leppin, 2010, pp. 104-106) Luther discussed the ideas behind university reform in his 1520 letter *To the Christian Nobility of the German Nation* (WA 6; AE 44). When the Reformation led to the closing of the cathedral and cloister schools that had been the locus of medieval schooling since Charlemagne, he and Melanchthon turned to grammar schools. Luther's first response was his 1524 letter *To The Councilmen of All Cities in Germany That They Establish and Maintain Christian Schools* (WA 15; AE 45), the Magna Charta of classical Christian education. Melanchthon's visits to the schools of Saxony led in 1528 to the publication of a model school plan, the *Instructions for Visitors* (WA 26; AE 40), that outlined a curriculum of catechesis in the faith, teaching the trivium beginning with Latin grammar, and reading the Two Canons. Under the leadership of men like Johannes Sturm in Strasburg and Johannes Bugenhagen in Scandinavia, this curriculum spread across Europe, including England. The results were an explosive growth in literacy among ordinary folk and artistic creativity in art, music, literature and science.

That Shakespeare was the product of a classical Christian education is often ignored, but the classical Christian roots of the Scientific Revolution are more often denied outright, as in such triumphs of American jurisprudence as Judge Jones's decision in Kitzmiller et al. v. Dover Area School District:

> Expert testimony reveals that since the scientific revolution of the sixteenth and seventeenth centuries, science has been limited to the search for natural causes to explain natural phenomena.... While supernatural explanations may be important and have merit they are not part of science.... This self-imposed convention of science which limits inquiry to testable, natural explanation about the natural world is referred to by philosophers as 'methodological naturalism,' and is sometimes known as the scientific method. (Jones, 2005)

Whenever "this self-imposed convention" arose, it was not during the Scientific Revolution. Historians of science know that both Christian theology and the classics influenced science in the sixteenth and seventeenth centuries. (Numbers, 2009) They tend, however, to study them as two separate sources instead of insisting that the decisive factor was the uniting of Christian and ancient thought, and the obvious source of this union of Christianity and the classics was the classical Christian education enjoyed by most educated people in that era.

The Scientific Revolution was self-consciously a return to the ideals and even the texts of ancient science. Copernicus knew that he was reviving the heliocentric hypothesis of Aristarchus of Samos from the third century BC. Andreas Vesalius based the foundational text of modern medicine, *De humani corporis fabrica*, on the second century AD Greek physician, Galen. It appeared in 1543, the same year Copernicus's *De revolutionibus* was published. "Like Copernicus, Vesalius presented his work as restoration of an ancient practice; also like Copernicus, he pointed out flaws in the work of his great model from antiquity; and like Copernicus the rationale for his project emerged directly from humanist values and ambitions." (Dear, 2009, p. 39) Historians often refer to this age as the Scientific Renaissance. The classical Christian curriculum these men studied continued to educate important scientists like Linnaeus in the Eighteenth century, Charles Darwin in the Nineteenth and Werner Heisenberg in the Twentieth.

Lutherans played a significant role in what they, like Copernicus and Vesalius, viewed as the restoration of ancient science. Georg Joachim Rheticus composed the first accessible description of Copernicus's ideas. As mathematics professor at Wittenberg in 1539, Rheticus visited Copernicus and in 1540 published *Narratio Prima* ("The First Account"). Lutheran theologian Andreas Osiander saw *De revolutionibus* through the press. His influential anonymous preface praised the work for "saving the phenomena," that is, providing a mathematical model that predicted the movement of the planets more elegantly than other models, without claiming the heliocentric system was physically real. Scholars in sixteenth century Wittenberg followed Osiander's lead and ignored the physical truth of Copernicus. They usually began their astronomy courses with a summary of Ptolemy's arguments for a stationary earth and then used Copernicus's model to make calculations of the movement of the celestial bodies. (Westman, 1975, pp. 164-193)

This was the method of Tycho Brahe, the greatest naked-eye observational astronomer who ever lived. His accurate observations cleared up many problems. His modification of the Ptolemaic model, with the sun circling the earth while the planets circled the sun, contended with Copernicus for generations. Among Lutheran scientists formed by the classical Christian curriculum, Johannes Kepler believed in Pythagoras and Plato as deeply as the Bible. He followed the arts of mathematics, even when they led him to postulate that the heavenly bodies moved in ellipses, instead of circles, an hypothesis denounced by the equally classical Galileo for breaking with a tradition traced to Plato of positing circular motion for the heavenly bodies. Kepler used geometry to describe the universe not only to "save the phenomena" but to give a true picture of the heavens, as Plato argued in Republic VI and the curriculum of Republic VII. Geometry haunted the seventeenth century. Thomas Hobbes called geometry "the only science God hath seen fit to bestow upon mankind." Newton composed *Principia* in Latin with geometrical proofs. The liberal arts were fundamental for the Scientific Revolution.

Classical Christian education was as central for the American Revolution as for the Reformation and the Scientific Revolution. When Henry Lee doubted the Declaration's originality, Jefferson denied he was attempting to be original. "It was intended to be an expression of the American mind.... All its authority rests then on the harmonizing sentiments of the day, whether expressed in conversation, in letters, printed essays, or in the elementary books of public right, as Aristotle, Cicero, Locke, Sidney, &c." (Jefferson and Peterson, 1984)

Jefferson's recollections are confirmed by other colonial activists. Jonathan Mayhew said in his 1766 sermon on the repeal of the Stamp Act, "Having been initiated in youth, in the doctrines of civil liberty, as they were taught by such men as Plato, Demosthenes, and Cicero, and other renowned persons among the ancients, and such as Sydney and Milton, Locke and Hoadley among the moderns; I liked them; they seemed rational." (Mayhew, 1766) In 1775 John Adams wrote to a Tory opponent, "These are what are called revolution principles. They are the principles of Aristotle and Plato, of Livy and Cicero, of Sidney, Harrington and Locke: the principles of nature and eternal reason." (Adams, 1851) Jefferson, Mayhew, and Adams traced "the doctrines of civil liberty," "the principles of nature and eternal reason," and the "authority" of the Declaration of Independence back to classical antiquity.

David Bederman points out the danger of ignoring the Founders' classical piety. (Bederman, 2008)

> It would be easy to dismiss the influence of the classical tradition on the Framing generation as some peculiar and pretentious residuum of the elite culture of the times. Indeed, in the modern historiography of the intellectual life of the early republic, that is precisely the prevalent view: that classicism was a mere window dressing to the pragmatic, hard-knuckled politics of the period. In the same fashion, these same historians have tended to discount the religious fervor of the times.... In accordance with this view, when the script of the Framing morality play veers off into unexpected pieces of dialogue—as when the Framers speak of God's providence and the role of churches in the new society, or of classical models of government and republican virtues—our modern, internal dramaturge excises these scenes, or, worse yet, annotates them as irrelevant.

Historian Clinton Rossiter gave the best praise of America's old classical education. (Rossiter, 1953, p. 22)

> It is easy to smile at the dull, rigid, crabbed methods that prevailed in colonial colleges, but if we judge the vineyards by the fruit they brought forth, we must acknowledge them a fertile ground of learning, science, reason, and liberty. They may not have taught young men enough useful knowledge, but they did teach them—in their own tradition-ridden way—to

think, communicate, and lead.... The roll call of Harvard and William and Mary men in the Revolution should be evidence enough that Latin, logic, and metaphysics were a rich fertilizer in the cultivation of reason, virtue, honor, and love of liberty.

It was not just the colonial period. In 2002 Caroline Winterer showed that classical education was the educational gold standard throughout the nineteenth century. (Winterer, 2002, p. 111) In 2009 Carl Richard's *Golden Age of Classics in America* demonstrated the classics' role in the rambunctious creativity and politics of antebellum America. (Richard, 2009, p. xii) After the Civil War, Richard argues, "the classics began a gradual decline due to social, economic and intellectual forces." I believe that the decline was very gradual until the cultural catastrophe of the 1960's. Episcopalian prep schools and Lutheran and Catholic parochial schools continued to teach Latin. According to the United States Office of Education, in school year 1889-1890, 34.7% of public high school students took Latin. In 1900 and 1910 one half of public high school students studied Latin. (Latimer, 1958, p. 26) More studied it in private and parochial schools. In 1962 there were still 728,637 students of high school Latin. (Goldberg, 1966)

The Founders knew that the classical Christian curriculum preserved a legacy of wisdom, justice and beauty that was essential for faith and freedom. As Rossiter saw, it had taughtthem and was to teach future generations of Americans to "think, communicate, and lead." They valued the Christian heritage as well. When Lutheran pastor Frederick Christian Schaeffer sent James Madison his sermon for the founding of St. Matthew's Church in New York City, Madison responded from retirement in Montpelier, Virginia (December 3, 1821), "Your address... illustrates the excellence of a system to which, by a due distinction, the genius and courage of Luther led the way, between what is due to Caesar and what is due God, best promotes the discharge of both obligations." (Madison, 1867) Classical Christian education remains what it was for the Founders, the best pedagogy for preparing Christians to live their vocations in God's two kingdoms with the blessings of political freedom and God's grace.

---

Dr. E. Christian Kopff, author of *The Devil Knows Latin: Why America Needs the Classical Tradition*, serves as associate professor of classics in the Honors program at the University of Colorado – Boulder.

## The Intent and Effect of American Progressive Education

*by Dr. Steven A. Hein*

Very few of us today are aware of the history of education in America. It is commonly thought that whatever innovations have come over the centuries and decades, they have been conceived and implemented with the goal of improving pedagogy to enable the learner to learn more and to learn more efficiently. Regardless of how the track record at any particular place or time is perceived, it is generally thought that the experts who have formulated innovations in the curriculum and methodology have done so with the goal of improving education for all our children – that is, to make our children better educated. Unfortunately this is not, and has never been, the case with compulsory, government-administered progressive American education whose beginnings can be traced to the middle 1800s in Boston, New York, and Philadelphia. The following overview has been gleaned largely from the well-documented treatment by educator John Gatto in *The Underground History of American Education.* (Gatto, 2001)

Our objective is to explore the factors that gave rise to progressive education in this country and to understand and appreciate its goals, methods, and results, especially during the 20th century. We seek to explorate these most basic questions: *Why educate? What are the goals and objectives that education is directed to accomplish with our children?* Only when we understand our educational goals and objectives are we in a position to evaluate any given approach.

It is concerning these basic questions that the roots of progressive education in our country, and indeed throughout the Western world, made a radical change during the middle of the 18th century beginning in Prussia. When the Prussian army went into a flawlessly executed battle engagement, after days of forced march to save Wellington from certain defeat by Napoleon at the battle of Waterloo, a surprised Western world took note. Prussia's understanding of how to train, manage, and execute a large military contingency to achieve a singular objective with coordinated precision, as set forth by field commanders, was quickly understood as to its applications of employing a grand labor force to push the industrial revolution into a new age of mass production.

First in Prussia, then in England and the United States, industrialization produced an enormous upheaval in national identity and purpose. Visionary industrialists, government officials, and educators began to understand the tremendous possibilities for mass production fueled by coal and later petroleum. Industrialization brought with it dreams of a utopian existence of endless material advances in the standard of American living. Coal and petroleum could fuel the production and operation of machines, factories, and assembly lines that could - with a rightly trained, efficient, mass labor force - crank out an endless array of inexpensively produced goods and gadgets that would eradicate poverty and disease, and that would also produce an unprecedented standard of living for all. It is important to understand the advantages envisioned and achieved for a mass society through successful schooling and social the adaption of a mass labor force during the hundred years from 1880s through the 1970s. In short, they comprise the physical comforts for all – food, shelter, cars, and TVs – with relative personal security, a predictable world with great freedom from anxieties of the unknowns in life.

In order for such a vision to be realized, a trade-off would be needed. The greater population of the country would have to be socialized and schooled to become an efficient, effective mass labor force to produce the goods and then consume them in pursuit of a life of better material living. Granted, the work would be largely strenuous, repetitive, and mindlessly boring – but it would promise job security, nice wages, and a chance to advance into a higher material standard of living. To provide for such a mass labor resource, an alliance between large corporate industrialists and Government would be necessary to raise up a compulsory schooling system. Designed to overturn the traditional task of educating our young for liberty and freedom, in order to enable them to make for themselves a life and career of their own choosing, this system would train students for social integration into a mass workforce for coordinated labor as prescribed, supervised, and evaluated by the production goals of higher management. The old enterprise of educating for critical and creative thought, problem solving, and communication would be retained partially, but not for the masses. Such education would become an elitist enterprise for only the brightest and best-connected children, a small minority who could take their places in government, the professions, and upper corporate management. For the masses, education for free thinking was seen as a clear threat and liability to realizing the collective utopian visions for reasons that we will make evident.

If the Christian vision is a life lived under the grace of the Savior Jesus Christ, a life of being a good steward, and a life serving Christ in the needs of one's neighbors, then the utopian vision responsible for compulsory government education conceptualized salvation as economic justice for the collective material betterment of mankind. No greater condition for man could be conceived. The good life was understood as a life of production and consumption, with an increasing array of material goods (add entertainment during the second half of the 20th century) to unprecedented standards of worldly living. The vision that brought us compulsory progressive education was often fueled with a religion-like zeal; but both the zeal and vision were decidedly rationalistic, shaped by Social Darwinism, Unitarian or atheist presuppositions, and thoroughly this-worldly. To accomplish the vision, the mental diet of children would have to undergo a radical change, and uniform compulsory government schooling could best accomplish this. The following elements would have to be neutralized or removed from the nurture of children. Note these carefully:

Facility in the language skills that enable critical thinking and speaking with others for persuasive interaction must be eliminated in all but the most gifted children who would need these skills for upper management, the professions, and state governance.

The traditional narrative of American history, that which connects the founding fathers and documents to the significant events of our nation's history so as to distinguish what it means to be American, would have to be deconstructed.

The traditional historical narrative would have to be substituted with a "social studies" regimen of simple uninterpreted facts, together with contemporary social values based on the materialist/consumption vision of the "good life."

Academic content of formal curriculum which familiarized students with serious literature, philosophy, and theology would need radical dilution in order to dampen any interest in economics, politics, or religion (esp. historic Christianity).

Replacement of phonics with whole language sight-word reading would be needed to remove the code-cracking drills that would otherwise allow self-mastery of reading skills for anyone.

Willing and unwilling students would need to be schooled and leveled off together, stratified by age.

Enlargement of the school day, days of the week, months of the year. and years in life spent in school would be necessary to retard the labor force, neutralize the drive and competitive spirit of young teen-aged children, and reduce the out-of-school influences on child formation in order to reduce useful knowledge for independent livelihoods.

Oversight from parents, church, community leaders, and students themselves would need to shift to bureaucratic school officials progressively more remote from the student's local world.

Progressive hostility would need to be expressed toward interpretative meanings shaped by religion. (Gatto, 2001, pp. 169-170)

Is this not simply educational reform intended to do things better? The new compulsory progressive education became a wholesale repudiation of the goals and means of traditional education, in an exchange for a scientifically designed mass schooling program. The goal was not to raise up educated citizens with intelligent, critical interaction with their lives and world, but rather to build a mass industrial labor force schooled for conformed efficiency. In the envisioned labor force, a traditionally educated person posed a threat to labor management and to cost-effective production. *Inculcating knowledge teaches workers to be able to perceive and calculate their grievances; thus, they become formidable foes in labor issues.* Moreover, The Report of the Senate Committee on Education in 1888 reported the following conclusion: *We believe that education is one of the principle causes of discontent of late years manifesting itself among the laboring classes....* (Gatto, 2001, p. 153)

The NEA came into existence to organize and shape the means and goals of molding and maintaining a teacher resource committed and equipped to implement the progressive program. The NEA's 1918 Report, Cardinal Principles of Secondary Education, decreed that *specified behaviors, health, and vocational training were the central goals of education, not mental development, not character, not godliness.* (Gatto, 2001, p. 108)

The strategy of gradualism effectively transformed American education into a monolithic compulsory, government-administered school system. The movement began in the east, especially in the cities of Boston, New York, and Philadelphia, in the middle decades of the 19th Century, traveled to the states in New England, moved to large cities like Chicago in the Midwest and to other larger urban centers, and finally to the rural states and regions of the country by the first half of the 20th century. Gradualism also progressively changed compulsory education laws. Dean of Education at Stanford, Elwood Cubberley, explained the strategy of gradualism in Public Education in the United States (1934):

At first the laws are optional . . . later the law was made state-wide, but the compulsory period was short (ten to twelve weeks) and the age limits low, not to twelve years. After this, struggle came to extend the time often little by little . . . to extend the age limits downward to eight and seven and upwards to fourteen, fifteen, or sixteen; to make the law apply to children attending private and parochial schools, and to require cooperation from such schools for the proper handling of cases; to institute state supervision of local enforcement; to connect school attendance enforcement with the child-labor legislation of the State through a system of working permits. (Gatto, 2001, p. 101)

The goals of progressive education, the institution and expansion of compulsory schooling, and restrictive child labor laws were all designed to achieve the same result – to intellectually dumb down and produce an efficient mass labor force, all while guarding against the greatest threat the utopian industrialists feared: overproduction, or what is more commonly called, *competition.* Shaped by a cartel of rich, visionary industrialists such as John D. Rockefeller, Andrew Carnegie, J. P. Morgan, and Henry Ford, the utopian program was fueled by those who feared risking the great capital of their enterprises' harnessing of coal, petroleum, and steel to a population of young educated and idealistic entrepreneurs. Imbued and equipped with a good education, entrepreneurs would be willing and able to build better and cheaper mousetraps or Model T horseless carriages that did not need a new model each year. If supplies increased, prices would drop, and capital could not be protected.

In the older, largely agrarian economy, parents toughened the minds of their own children through education in serious literature, writing, debate, and competence in managing numbers. Education began in this manner in young childhood to foster the early desire and appreciation of independence and creativity. But such an educated young person was just what was feared. The new utopian vision included curtailing the labor of young people, keeping them in schools for longer days – and longer years of their development – as this would deprive them of an educated, creative mind and the means to apply it in the market place during their most energetic and idealistic years. (Remember the shorter life expectancy for Americans 100-150 years ago.) Prior to coal-fired mass production, the notion of using one's education to enter one's own business enterprise was seen as the most positive exercise of freedom and liberty for American youth. During colonial days in America, if a young man had not established a successful business as an entrepreneurial tradesman by the age of 13 or 14, he was considered a failure and would probably need to become what was considered the most derogatory work classification at the time – *a common laborer.*

The connection was both simple and inescapable. Adam Smith's understanding of a market run by self-regulating competition would be the death of the planned, managed economy. The presence of independently minded, well-educated Americans had to be curtailed. Excessive overproduction of brains was understood as the root cause of the overproduction of virtually anything and everything. When some raised doubts in the middle of the 20th century, James Bryant Conan (President of Harvard, 1935-53) wrote a defense of the new program in The American High School Today. For Conan, progressive education was a triumph of Anglo/Germanic pragmatism, as it brilliantly curtailed the American entrepreneurial spirit for perfectly justifiable reasons. If capital investments were vulnerable to millions of young, self-reliant, educated, and resourceful entrepreneurs, no one would risk the huge amounts of capital necessary to create or sustain the new commercial/industrial/financial machine of mass production. The whole enterprise would have never begun, or would have soon collapsed. (Gatto, 2001, p. 321) Consider John D. Rockefeller's 1906 General Education Board document, Occasional Letter Number One:

In our dreams . . . people yield themselves with perfect docility to our molding hands. The present educational conventions [intelligent and character education] fade from our minds, and unhampered by tradition we work our own good will upon a grateful and responsive folk. We shall not try to make these people or any of their children into philosophers, or men of learning or men of science. We have not to raise up from among them authors, educators, poets or men of letters. We shall not search for embryo great artists, painters, musicians, nor lawyers, doctors, preachers, politicians, statesmen, of whom we have ample supply. The task we set before ourselves is simple . . . we will organize children . . . and teach them to do in a perfect way the things their fathers and mothers are doing in an imperfect way . . . . (Gatto, 2001, p. 45)

## A Closer Look at the Impact of Progressive Education on Reading

There has been a consensus down through the centuries – unchallenged by progressive schooling proponents – that attentive reading of tough-minded writing that wrestles with central challenges of human existence is the best, fastest, and cheapest way known for learning to think analytically and independently. Serious reading with rigorous discussion of content requires the development of critical thinking, articulate speaking, and the mastery of human language. Learning how to read and argue form the foundation of a solid education for a learned and literate citizenry. Nowhere was progressive schooling more devastating than in the area of reading. In 1812, prior to progressive education, barely four in a thousand Americans could *not* read proficiently. The key to retarding intellectually its future mass labor force would be to restrict its ability to read. This would be accomplished by changing how reading would be taught, and also by changing what would be read.

The ancient Greeks made the astounding discovery centuries before that had advanced the ability to read and master language. They created letters to represent language sounds. Learning sight-sound correspondences is easy. The naming of sounds, rather than things, was an incredible breakthrough. Communicating abstractions in picture language requires, for most people, much more time and training than communicating with letters and words. The Greeks created words with combinations of sounds, and they understood that proper syntactical writing would lead to construction of phrases and sentences capable of conveying even the most complex, abstract ideas.

The Romans made it even easier by naming the letters closely with the sound of the letters. Christian missionaries adapted the Roman alphabet to English (not very easily) in the 7th century, and the rest, as they say, is history. For a long time there was not much to read in English, as Latin was the academic language of learning. The King James Version of the Bible became the universal textbook in early American education. Learning the alphabet and its phonetic sounds, and then decoding words in the Bible, became the most popular way that children among all social classes – rich and poor – quickly learned to read. As children learned to read and master the most complex sentences and vocabulary at the earliest of ages, they were constantly rewarded and motivated to learn more as they became more enlightened about the fundamental questions of human existence everyone is interested in: *What is life? What is death? How can the future can be secured by a loving and merciful Creator and Redeemer?*

Not surprisingly, it was a German disciple of Rousseau who published in 1791 the first look/say reading primer, through which students would learn words through pictures. (Gatto, 2001, p. 64) (I can remember my first reading lesson using pictures to teach word association – the method we now call *whole language or word instruction*. It was the first grade and there was the corresponding picture on a large easel with the words: *Look baby, see the water.*) Horace Mann and his wife Mary Peabody promoted this word picture reading method as Thomas Gallaudet had set it forth in his sight-reading program for the deaf. (Gatto, 2001, p. 67) Learning to read in this way (you certainly could not use phonics!) taught deaf children how to speak. The first line in the primer was *Frank had a dog; his name was Spot*. But Mann and later progressive educators sought to adopt the pictorial whole-language approach to teach reading to children who had no hearing difficulties and who already had considerable facility in spoken language. He battled the Boston School authorities until his death in efforts to bring Gallaudet's whole language approach to reading to Boston. Said Mann, *I am satisfied our greatest error in teaching children to read lies in beginning with the alphabet.* (Gatto, 2001, p. 69) It wasn't until the crusade for whole language by Francis Parker and other reading antagonists in the 1880s that the push succeeded with the help of a psychologist, James McKeen Cattell. Cattell conducted an experiment with a contraption called a *tachistoscope* that allegedly proved *we read whole words and not letters*. It was not until 1965 that anyone bothered to check his experiment and discovered that he was dead wrong. People read letters, not words. Indeed, reports Gatto, there were 124 legitimate studies performed from 1911 to 1981 attempting to prove Cattell and other whole-word advocates right. None of the studies confirmed whole word reading as effective. (Gatto, 2001, pp. 70, 73)

Nevertheless, the progressive adoption of the whole-language approach to reading promised just the needed wholesale means to retard children's learning, and it also eventually provided the financial bonanza to textbook publishing companies that led to the famous (or infamous) *Dick and Jane* reading series. Now, for several generations of reading, it would be *Dick had a dog named Spot*. By 1920 sight reading had begun to replace phonics as the standard method of teaching reading in American government-sponsored education, and by the 1930s the *Dick and Jane* series was becoming the most popular whole-language reading series. Over the next twenty years, the series was progressively dumbed-down further. In 1930, the Dick and Jane pre-primer taught only 68 sight words in 39 pages of story text, one illustration per page, for a total of 565 words. Its Teacher's Guidebook had 87 pages. By 1951 (when I entered the world of Dick and Jane), the same book taught only 58 sight words, yet it had expanded to 172 pages of text, 184 illustrations, and contained a total of 2,603 words. The Teacher's Guidebook had swelled to 182 pages – all this to teach 58 words! *In 1930, the word "look" appears 8 times; in 1951, 110 times. In 1930, "oh" repeats 12 times; in 1951, 138 times. In 1930, "see" has 27 repetitions compared with 176 in 1951.* (Gatto, 2001, p. 72) Contrast also the content of Dick and Jane with the content of the King James Version of the Bible. Instead of reading about the great Noachian flood, the battle between David and Goliath, and the crucifixion of Jesus, children learned a few dozen bland words repeated - *ad nauseum* - with a color picture on each page. "Look, look, look." The books explored such mind-emptying drivel as Dick and Spot going to the grocery store, Spot spilling some milk, and Officer Friendly walking them back home. The famous Dr. Seuss of *Cat in the Hat* fame put the mindlessness of all this before the public in an interview he gave in 1981:

> I did it for a textbook house and they sent me a word list. That was due to the Dewey revolt in the twenties, in which they threw out phonics reading and went to word recognition as if you're reading a Chinese pictograph instead of blending sounds or different letters. I think killing phonics was one of the greatest causes of illiteracy in the country. . . . Anyway they had it all worked out that a healthy child at the age of four can only learn so many words in a week. So there were two hundred and twenty-three words to use in this book. I read the list three times and I almost went out of my head. I said, "I'll read it once more and if I can find two words that rhyme, that'll be the title of my book." I found cat and hat and said

the title of my book will be "The Cat in the Hat." (Gatto, 2001, p. 73)

In 1840, records from Connecticut and Massachusetts revealed that virtually everyone could read, and at a very proficient level, with almost no formal schooling in terms of months in the year or years of one's youth. In 1940, one hundred years later, only 4% of whites and 20% of blacks were illiterate. Just sixty years later, by the year 2000, white illiteracy had quadrupled to 12% and black illiteracy had doubled to 40%. During these sixty years, education expenditures increased 400%. Between 1955 and 1991, the annual expense per student increased 350%, teacher compensation increased by 50%, all while student/teacher ratios decreased by 40%. (Gatto, 2001, pp. 52-55) In 1993, the National Adult Literacy Survey surveyed 190 million U.S. adults over the age of 16. Despite an average school attendance of 12.4 years, the following results emerged from these 190 million:

Forty-two million Americas over the age of 26 could not read.

Fifty million Americans could recognize printed words on a 4th or 5th grade level, but could not write simple messages or letters.

Fifty-five million Americans were limited to 6th-8th grade reading levels. A majority of this group could not figure out the price per ounce of peanut butter in a 20-ounce jar costing $1.99, even when told they could round the answer to a whole number.

Only 30 million Americans possessed 9th or 10th grade level reading proficiency. This group (and all of the previous) could not understand a simplified written explanation of the procedures used by attorneys and judges to select juries.

Only 3.5% were deemed to have reading proficiency ready to begin college work, contrasted with 30% of all high school students in 1940.

96.5% of this American adult population was considered mediocre to illiterate where deciphering print is concerned; they must rely on others to tell them what things reported about their world mean. (Gatto, 2001, pp. 61-62)

## Some Reflections

In light of the question: *Why educate?*, how might we assess the history of progressive government-sponsored compulsory schooling, especially during the 20th century? In response to criticisms about the mediocrity of the American public school system, Walter Green protested *the myth of our failing schools* in 1998, in the *Atlantic Monthly,* on the following grounds:

We just happen to have the world's most productive work force, the largest economy, the highest material standard of living, more Nobel prizes than the rest of the world combined, the best system of higher education, the best high-tech medicine, and the strongest military. These things could not have been accomplished with second-rate systems of education. (Gatto, 2001, p. 151)

The paradox is that only by a second-rate educational system could these things have been produced - especially considering what was accomplished prior to 1980. The progressives' school system did create an effective, efficient mass labor force that harnessed the energy of coal and petroleum to produce a standard of material living never before reached in the history of the world. The program worked, especially given that the third world had yet to industrialize, and European western economies were decimated by two world wars during the first half of the 20th century. However, John Gatto notes Green's confusion between education and schooling. Our material prosperity, affluence, and power came about through schooling, not through first-rate education.

> The truth is that America's unprecedented global power and spectacular material wealth is a direct product of a third-rate educational system, upon whose inefficiency in developing intellect and character it depends. If we educated better we could not sustain the corporate utopia we have made. Schools build national wealth by tearing down personal sovereignty, morality, and family life. It's a trade off. (Gatto, 2001, p. 151)

The continuing problem has been the virtual ignorance about the goals and objectives we have outlined above, those that form the rationale behind progressive schooling as it was established and matured throughout the 20th century. The major resistance to the program as it began and first evolved from the east to the west, from the urban centers to the rural hamlets, were parents. For the most part, they were out-resourced by educators, industrialists, and government officials, and they lost nearly every battle. Unwittingly and tragically, many influential religious leaders in the American Protestant denominations enthusiastically endorsed the establishment of the legal foundations for government-sponsored, compulsory education as a counter to the Roman Catholic school system and its influence. There is perhaps no better place where this alliance between secular utopians and Protestant Churchmen finally achieved a complete victory over the civic influences of its Roman Catholic constituency than in the city of San Francisco during the 20th century. It is what it is today, in part, by the eradication of longstanding Roman Catholic influence in its culture and politics.

Most generations of regular folk, especially after the Second World War, have been completely ignorant of the history of American education. The common belief held by most parents and teachers is that the innovations that have come on the scene in the name of educational reform have been advanced for the sake of improving the effectiveness of educating our children. This simply is not the case. The old education, its strategies, and methods were not replaced by a system of compulsory schooling designed to do the job of educating our children in a superior or more effective manner. It was quite the opposite! The purpose of the compulsory, government-sponsored schooling system was to retard and to dumb-down learning, to restrict the educated classes to the brightest and best, and to relegate the rest of American children to becoming compliant laborers to produce and consume ever increasing quantities of our own manufactured goods. Now, after years of this system, we produce little (mostly services, including entertainment), and we are not competing effectively in today's global economy.

Today, our schools are the product of startling incompetency due to both the vacuum of a bygone industrial age and the paralyzing power of teachers' unions. We no longer have the factories and mills that require a mass labor force. Since the close of the 1970s, the productive energies of American industrialization and the dream utopia have declined rapidly. The baby-boomer generation, which received from American mass production energies possibly the greatest increase of material blessing over against the previous generation, found the whole utopian enterprise to be completely unfulfilling. They started a protest during the hippy generation in the 1960s and early 1970s, and they pronounced the verdict that a life of great material prosperity and consumption was empty, hollow, and hostile to the human spirit. In order to cope with the intellectual and spiritual vacuum of a materialist culture and a third-rate education, they turned not to better and more traditional education, but to drugs, sex, and entertainment - continuing staples of contemporary escapist culture.

Conclusion

This most fundamental question must be raised before anyone can evaluate different pedagogies: *Why educate?* If you are not clear on why your children should be educated – to what end – you are not yet in a position to evaluate how and where they should be educated. We have seen that the answer to this essential question underwent a radical change from previous time periods in Western and American history, shaped by the materialistic utopian visions and objectives of 19th progressive industrialists and educators. Today, we now face a tremendous need for Christian parents, pastors, and educators to think through this question very carefully. For the Christian, education of our children is an extension of life lived under the grace of the Savior Jesus Christ, a life of being a good steward, and a life serving Christ in the needs of one's neighbors. When we answer correctly the question, *Why educate?*, we can then establish clear priorities and make beneficial decisions about where and how our baptized children should be educated.

---

Dr. Hein is an affiliate faculty member at Patrick Henry College. Founding member of the Consortium for Classical and Lutheran Education, he serves as Director of the Concordia Institute for Christian Studies.

Notes

# III. Teaching Content in Classical Lutheran Education

Notes

## Teaching the *Quadrivium*

*by Jackquelyn Veith*

Many classical Lutheran educators, whether in a school or home environment, have become excited to rediscover the classical liberal arts and sciences. We especially appreciate the use of the trivium as a framework to teach our students and children; however, the purpose of classical education is to teach our students to reason, to recognize, and to defend the truth. The trivium's framework is just a beginning. In fact, the classical liberal arts and sciences are far more than just the trivium!

The *Classical Education* figure presents a model of classical education demonstrating that the seven liberal arts are divided into two groups, the trivium and the quadrivium. The arts of the trivium deal with language; the arts of the quadrivium deal with mathematics. All of the arts develop intellectual skills and abilities to apply to the three branches of knowledge: moral, natural, and theological sciences. Without all of these arts and sciences, a classical education is incomplete.

Since the Enlightenment, knowledge has been taught as increasingly isolated and fragmented. Classical education, however, presents knowledge as integrated.

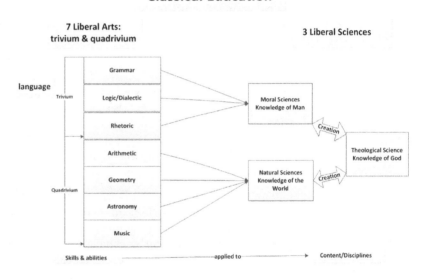

Figure 1: Classical Education

Even the seemingly "new" areas such as computer science or sociology fall within a classical education taxonomy. For example content found in the STEM realms of science, technology, engineering, and mathematics, apply within the quadrivium.

Classical and Lutheran educators have focused solidly on developing curricula and schools in order to implement the classical arts of the trivium: grammar, logic, and rhetoric. Incorporation of the classical quadrivial arts is not so strongly evident.

Perhaps one reason the quadrivium has been neglected can be traced to Dorothy L. Sayer's implication in "The Lost Tools of Learning," that the quadrivium refers merely to subjects or content areas. Some classical Christian school leaders who trace their roots to her influential essay have subsequently classified the quadrivium accordingly. Furthermore, based also on overly narrow inferences from this essay, some apply the trivium solely as pedagogical stages in a developmental framework. Douglas Wilson, author of *Recovering the Lost Tools of Learning*, and the Association of Christian Classical Schools[2], serve at times as examples based upon this understanding. Robert Littlejohn and Charles Evans caution against an over reliance on the developmental approach and provide a broader view:

> We champion, as did Sayers and the ancients, the integration of all the disciplines and the need to purposefully teach our students skills that are readily transferable to other disciplines. We herald, with her, the importance of emphasizing rudimentary knowledge and skills with our youngest students, but we flatly deny that there is any historical precedent or practical necessity for a construct such as 'the grammar of history' or 'the grammar of mathematics.' Because the liberal arts constitute seven foundational disciplines, each with its own rudiments and complexities, we could as readily recommend that students be taught 'the astronomy of rhetoric'....While it may be clever or whimsical to use such expressions figuratively, the serious use of such constructs undermines the integrity of the liberal arts disciplines. Overall, we believe that the concept has proven far more confusing than useful. (Littlejohn and Evans, 2006, p. 39)

For Luther and Melanchthon, the trivium alone was not enough. Martin Luther wrote, "I would have them study not only languages and history, but also singing and music together with the whole of mathematics." Melanchthon recognized that the lower arts – grammar, logic, rhetoric – paved "the way for knowing the higher arts." Luther and Melanchthon understood the need for both the trivium and quadrivium, and they drew from their own educations in the liberal arts and sciences the classical curricula in schools they founded. (Korcok, 2011, pp. 72, 76)

The foci and purposes of both the trivium and quadrivium are necessary. The trivium focuses on language and prepares the student to understand and think in words; the quadrivium focuses on numbers and prepares the student to understand and think in numbers. Students need to be able to think logically, reason mathematically, and communicate clearly. One classical source regarding the quadrivium is Boethius (480-524 A.D.) who described the quadrivium as the study of number and its relationship to physical space or time. According to his description, mathematics is "pure number," geometry is "number in space," music is "number in time," and astronomy is "number in space and time."

Sister Miriam Joseph contrasted the quadrivium to the trivium in this way: the trivium focuses on language and pertains to the mind, while the quadrivium focuses on numbers and pertains to matter. The "four arts of quantity" can be either discrete (mathematics and music) or continuous (geometry and astronomy). Two theoretical arts (mathematics and geometry) relate to arts of application (music and astronomy). Each of the liberal arts has come to be understood not in the narrow sense of a single subject but rather in the sense of a group of related subjects. The quadrivium comprises not only mathematics but also many branches of science, so the theory of space includes the study of analytic geometry and analytic trigonometry. Applications of the theory of space include principles of architecture, geography, surveying, and engineering. (Miriam and McGlinn, 2002)

More contemporary explanations are provided by Morris Kline, Gene Veith, and Andrew Kern. Kline, an American mathematician, describes the quadrivial arts in a modernist way: arithmetic is "pure,"

---

[2]The Association of Classical Christian Schools website http://www.accsedu.org

geometry is "stationary," music is "applied," and astronomy is "moving." (Kline, 1953) Veith and Kern explain mathematics as "abstract and absolute thought," geometry as "relationships of objects in space," music as "aesthetic perception," and astronomy as "observation and study." (Veith and Kern, 2001) This chart summarizes these explanations:

|  | Boethius | Sister Miriam Joseph | Kline | Veith & Kern |
|---|---|---|---|---|
| Mathematics | Pure Number | Theory of Number, discrete | Pure | Abstract & absolute thought |
| Geometry | Number In Space | Theory of Space, continuous | Stationary | Relationsships of objects in space |
| Music | Number In Time | Application of theory of number, discrete | Applied | Aesthetic perception |
| Astronomy | Number In Space And Time | Application of theory of space, continuous | Moving | Observation & study |

What are the consequences of neglecting the quadrivium? Based on high standardized test scores, surely educating by the trivium can be deemed "good enough", but if we want our students to think intelligently, we must give them all of the essential mental tools. The quadrivium prepares our students to reason in a different way than does the trivium.

Students from Patrick Henry College recently described the consequences of neglecting the quadrivium:

> "People educated only in the trivium cannot talk in a Science, Technology, Engineering and Math-oriented world. The current emphasis on STEM needs a classical answer besides just 'we do words.'"

> "Students with a talent for math and science may reject a trivium-heavy approach because their interests have no place in it or what they are assigned."

> "Would a non-believer get a different answer for 1 + 1? Objective truth is true no matter what worldview is taught!"

What are the obstacles to teaching the quadrivium as it should be taught? Continued misunderstanding and a lack of knowledge definitely contribute to the barriers. Mathematics as a thinking process, not just a content area, may be very difficult for those of us without classical education to appreciate. Moreover, many available math curricula lack the classical approach. We concentrate strongly on the basics of math, but what are we doing to prepare students for more advanced levels of math? How are students prepared to connect their mathematical knowledge to other disciplines and arts? In this day of the internet and quantum knowledge, the sheer volume of material to teach in a limited amount of time can be daunting.

Nonetheless, efforts must be made beginning at the youngest age. These suggestions for teaching the quadrivium are offered for consideration (Littlejohn and Evans, 2006, p. 39):

- Teach the theory as well as the practical knowledge at age-appropriate levels and with clear mathematical vocabulary.

- Explain what students will need to know and how they will integrate this knowledge in the future.

- Connect their learning to what they already know and point to what they will learn.

- Give them the "big picture" as well as the age-appropriate details.

- Highlight the historical connections and the philosophy behind the content areas of the quadrivium.

- Explain the integrated nature of learning: poetry is the mathematical relationship of words; music is the mathematical relationship of sounds.

- Apply the trivium as methodology to the quadrivium: prepare students for future learning through scaffolding (grammar); as students practice applying absolutes (logic), decrease the scaffolding until the student can independently recognize and apply absolutes (rhetoric).

- Borrow from Vygotsky's Zone of Proximal Development and Bloom's Taxonomy to spiral up the rigor of instruction, assignments, and assessments.

As classical Lutheran educators with a strong appreciation for the trivium, let us take the lead in studying, preparing, and developing resources for the quadrivium. As we share quadrivial curricula, students will benefit. Our society needs citizens who can solve problems and think quantitatively. Our Lutheran schools, homes, and churches will be strengthened by students who have been taught to recognize, appreciate, and defend absolute truths.

---

Mrs. Jackquelyn Veith, M.S. in Curriculum and Instruction, is Director of Assessment for Patrick Henry College. Wife of Dr. Gene Edward Veith, mother of three, and grandmother of eight, Mrs. Veith serves as Executive Director for Educational Certification with the Consortium for Classical and Lutheran Education.

## Musical Literacy

*by Tevia Grimenstein*

> Musical training is a more potent instrument than any other, because rhythm and harmony find their way into the inward places of the soul, on which they mightily fasten, imparting grace, and making the soul of him who is rightly educated graceful, or of him who is ill-educated ungraceful... (Plato and Jowell, 2000, p. 73)

Arithmetic, Geometry, Astronomy, and . . . Music? The Quadrivium is a curious beast. The Greeks believed music to be more than important; music was heavenly. Indeed, the heavens themselves produce music – the "music of the spheres." Music exerts great power over man. More than imitating the emotions of the soul, music also transforms the soul. (Grout et al., 1960, p. 8) So vital was this understanding to the Greeks that in the constitutions of their city-states they regulated musical composition and controlled the musical activities of their citizens. (Grout et al., 1960, p. 9)

Music is neither "elective" nor merely supplemental to other disciplines. Rather, music works with all of the liberal arts to cultivate wholeness in the educated student. (Martineau, 2010, p. 3) Consider a 12th-century drawing by French theologian Alain de Lille. Entitled "Grammar," the drawing depicts Grammar as unlocking the door to proper instruction. In the balconies rest the remaining liberal arts, all highly regarded: Logic, Rhetoric, Arithmetic, Music, Geometry, and Astronomy. At the very top sits Theology – the "Queen of Sciences" – overseeing all knowledge. The drawing illustrates the classical belief in the necessity of all seven liberal arts. (Martineau, 2010, p. 3)

Figure 2: Queen of Sciences

Fully implemented, classical education produces musical literacy. Just as a mathematician seeks to understand the true nature of numbers and an astronomer the true nature of the heavens, so a musician pursues the true nature of music. Medieval music theorist Guido d'Arezzo wrote of this pursuit when he said, "...he who does what he does not understand is termed a beast." (Pesce, 2010, p. 25)

### An Ancient Affinity for Music

Common classical references, with such figures as Apollo, Pan, and Orpheus, depict the Greeks' high regard of music. The god of light and music, young Apollo possessed a prized voice which "rose above all the others." (D'Aularie and DAulaire, 1962, p. 42) As god of nature, Pan played "sweet and unearthly" melodies on his shepherd's pipe. (D'Aularie and DAulaire, 1962, p. 90) Mortal son of the Muse Calliope, Orpheus left his home to bring the joy of music to earth. His voice "rang so pure and true that the fiercest warriors put down their swords and savage beasts lay spellbound at his feet. Trees pulled up their roots and moved closer to listen, and even hard rocks rolled up to him." (D'Aularie and DAulaire, 1962, p. 101) Indeed, the music of Orpheus opened even the gates of Hades! (D'Aularie and DAulaire, 1962, p. 102)

Figure 3: Music

The story to explain music's inclusion in the Quadrivium is not a legend about gods or heroes; rather, the story involves a Greek mathematician and a blacksmith. According to legend, Pythagoras one day passed Tubalcain's blacksmith shop and heard harmonies resonating from the anvils. When Pythagoras observed that each blacksmith used a different-sized anvil, he hurried back to his study to experiment with bells, strings, and flutes. Pythagoras determined that ratio and number were responsible for pleasing, consonant musical sounds. (Grout et al., 1960, p. 6) In another 12th-century drawing by Alain de Lille entitled "Music," blacksmith Tubalcain in the upper right pounds hammer to anvil, while below him mathematician Pythagoras balances hammers and bells.

Few people associate Pythagoras with music, although many consider his contributions to mathematics, as with the Pythagorean Theorem. Pythagoras, however, established Greek musical thought in 500 B.C. (Grout et al., 1960, p. 6) Furthermore, Pythagoras proposed a thorough education in disciplines related to one another by number. Arithmetic (number), Geometry (number in space), and Astronomy (number in space and time) require mathematical understanding. Likewise, Music involves the study of number, but in relation to time. (Martineau, 2010, p. 3) In the early days of the Quadrivium, this study was called harmonics, and harmonics became the essence of Greek music education.

Not until later in Greek history did the Greeks attribute to music great moral and philosophical power. In *The Republic*, Plato concluded that if music and astronomy were akin in their relation to time, then music must have heavenly properties. Both he and Aristotle envisioned a two-fold education for the heroes of Greece: gymnastics for the body and music for the soul. (Plato and Jowell, 2000, p. 48) Plato established laws – musical laws - for the proper use of harmony and rhythm to express sorrow, joy, penitence, or courage. These laws were not to be changed for fear of "lawlessness in art and education" (Grout et al., 1960, p. 8) He wrote, "When a beautiful soul harmonizes with a beautiful form, and the two are cast in one mould, that will be the fairest of sights to him who has an eye to see it." (Plato and Jowell, 2000, p. 74) Classical music education achieves a love of true beauty.

### Repetite, Repetite, Repetite

Despite the consensus through ancient times and the Middle Ages that music elevated the character and provided a vital component in the education of the young, disputes arose as to the proper method of music instruction. Musical theorists proposed that since music was a science of numbers, the numbers should be taught to children. Pictures such as the Bonaventura Hand helped children memorize complex mathematical relationships in music. Music teachers, however, argued that complex theory instruction was difficult and passive. They proposed a more active music instruction involving musical dialogue – repetition and imitation. (Murray, 2010, p. 304)

Grammar instruction during this time consisted of music education along with phonics in both the student's native language and in Latin. Very young children learned to sing by repeating what the teacher sang to them. Beginning with the physical property of sound, music education taught children to "play" their vocal instruments. The children sang simple songs, propers, ordinaries, and psalm tones. As they progressed in the ability to read texts, students learned from their teachers the physical reading of music with a song and a slate. Children both repeated what the teacher sang and copied the written music, as music theory entered the realm of the classroom. (Haar, 2010, p. 7) Eventually, students achieved musical literacy as they mastered each element: scales, the interval of unison, advanced intervals, intervals of octave, major key signatures, relationships between the keys, relative minor keys, and finally melodic and harmonic minor scales. (Haar, 2010, p. 6)

Repetition and imitation became hallmarks of classical music education, and these formed the foundation of music instruction throughout the Middle Ages and beyond. J.S. Bach received his formal music instruction from a teacher who encouraged him to sing, copy, and perform. (Bukofzer, 1947, p. 407) His early compositions were adaptations of great musical works. Even in his later life as a composer, Bach continued to copy the masters. A most beautiful example of this practice is his 12 Organ Concertos for Vivaldi. In these pieces, Bach transcribed twelve of Antonio Vivaldi's violin concertos for organ, imitating so delicately as to merely hint at the original pieces.

Bach's own students adhered to a strict curriculum of copying and writing. (Bukofzer, 1947, p. 407) After his students learned early elements of music theory, they imitated and repeated. In this manner, Bach taught his students counterpoint, the relationship between musical lines which move independently but when played together sound harmonious. Pietro Pontio, a medieval music theorist, said, "Counterpoint is the beginning and the road that leads to compositions, since from there come later many beautiful and varied compositions." (Murray, 2010, p. 307) Through the study of counterpoint, students examine the validity of a musical argument, so to speak – the logic of the sound. Again, this study is executed by repeating and imitating increasingly complex interval patterns and compositions. (Bukofzer, 1947, p. 310)

Classical music education produces not only musical literacy and a love of true beauty, but it also produces music. After students grasp both the basic elements of music theory and engage in analysis of music, they begin to compose. Composition, the true end of classical music education, is to music as rhetoric is to language. The common thought of the Middle Ages was that a performer was a "mere practitioner". (Pesce, 2010, p. 25) In contrast, the true musician understood music sufficiently to judge both composition and performance; moreover, he composed beautiful music.

## For the Love of Music

As Lutherans, we enjoy a rich musical heritage of liturgical worship. From infancy the sounds of organs and hymns, canticles and psalmodies surround us. Whether in the classical and Lutheran school or home school, music is both necessary and feasible to teach.

In the Middle Ages, children began their musical instruction by singing. Likewise, a homeschooler who brings her children weekly to the Divine Service and sings with them offers initial instruction in the discipline of music. A Lutheran school with daily worship gives children beginning opportunities to produce beautiful sounds with their voices. In either setting, within our own Lutheran liturgy and hymnody, the foundation for future music studies is laid.

As learning continues, parents or school teachers can introduce complex aspects of music theory. Children learn from a curriculum or, if the instructor is especially knowledgeable in music, through dialogue and imitation. Good examples of this include the hand signals of Solfege (do, re, mi, etc.) and the circle of fifths. Hand signals are akin to manipulatives and physically involve the children in memorable ways. Likewise, the introduction and memorization of the circle of fifths is no different than the introduction and memorization of multiplication tables. As the child grasps the concepts of music, he will begin to analyze the hymns, for example, that he sings. He also prepares to grapple with logical questions he may have about the music he encounters: How does a beautiful melody move? How do lines of harmony relate to melody? Why does melody seem to come to a rest or conclusion?

Any fear of teaching music can be overcome when we compare it to a more accessible discipline like mathematics, in which the early use of teddy bear counters helps the child to visualize structure and patterns. When a child names a pattern of blue-red-blue-red bears in mathematics as A-B-A-B, he becomes familiar with the concept of letter substitution. As the child grows, he experiments with basic algebraic formulas: $3 + X = 7$. The child knows that $X = 4$, so the child becomes comfortable solving equations with variables. Later when he encounters a more complex equation, such as $2X + 3 = Y$, he remembers his earlier experiences, and his knowledge enables him to learn how to solve something new.

Similarly, consider the young music student and a series of two musical notes. A high note, "A," is assigned to a red teddy bear. A low note, "B," is the blue teddy bear. As the child listens to the two notes, he places the bears in the order in which the notes are played. Today our melody is A-B-A – just three notes: high, low, high.

Later, the child sings "Twinkle, Twinkle, Little Star". The teacher designates the entire first line "Twinkle, Twinkle, Little Star..." as the letter A. "Up above the world so high..." becomes the letter B. When prompted, the child sings each section. After he sings the song in its entirety, he recognizes the repeated line A at the end. He names the melody A-B-A. The child has now learned the "rondo" form!

As he continues to practice the A-B-A pattern with other songs or improvised melodies, he becomes so familiar with the form that he recognizes the pattern even in the Kyrie or Te Deum. When the child listens to his first symphony and is introduced to the basic structure of exposition (melody), development, and recapitulation (reprise of the exposition), he discovers that it is rondo form. The teacher replies, "Yes, a very sophisticated rondo form, but still ABA." The child now comprehends the patterns, structure, and beauty of music.

It is important to note that not all students will be inclined toward music – just as not all students are inclined toward mathematics, history, or Latin. The composer Josquin des Pres, whom Luther described as a "master of the notes," believed in limiting the teaching of composition (advanced musical studies) to students who were "drawn to this delightful art by natural impulse." (Murray, 2010, p. 306) This may mean that the classical Lutheran school or home school teaches music in more fundamental and analytical ways to all, but then reserves advanced musical studies for the student who displays the desire or aptitude to be a musician. The older student inclined toward the study of music is assisted by his classical Lutheran school or home school in more elevated studies. Nonetheless, the younger child who learns only to sing and achieves but a basic understanding of music will find that his study of music benefits himself and the church.

### A Final Word: Vocation

Dr. Gene Edward Veith encourages Lutheran educators to assist students as they prepare for their future vocations. He writes, "Preparing for a calling involves self-knowledge, the discovery of talents, and the cultivation of interests." (Veith, 2011, p. 102) Without a strong music curriculum, the young classical

Lutheran student may be deprived of understanding his own musical inclinations, discovering his musical talents, or cultivating his musical interest.

Today in North Carolina, the author's dear friend, an experienced organist, prepares for retirement. With carpal tunnel syndrome and failing eyesight, she is ready to retire, but there is no one to replace her. Our current drought of church musicians has resulted from our failure to encourage and engage students in the true study of music.

The classical Lutheran school and home school bear responsibility for the future of our church's music. Given the opportunity to master music, our students may become organists, Kantors, liturgists, or hymn writers. Classical and Lutheran music is an essential liberal art with the precise structure and inherent ability to produce musically literate students able to serve their neighbors and the church.

---

Tevia Grimenstein, Bachelor of Music from Illinois Wesleyan University, is wife of Reverend Edward Grimenstein (M.A. Classical Rhetoric, M.Div. Concordia Theological Seminary in Ft. Wayne, and Th.D. Homiletics), classical Lutheran homeschooler and mother of their six children.

Notes

## Towards a More Humble Science

*by Dr. Ross Betts*

> We will restore science to its rightful place and wield technology's wonders to raise health care's quality and lower its cost. We will harness the sun and the winds and the soil to fuel our cars and run our factories. And we will transform our schools and colleges and universities to meet the demands of a new age. *-Barack Obama*

The proper role of science in public life is of considerable concern to both progressives and traditionalists. Many progressives, perhaps like our president, are reluctant to concede that there are roles for philosophy, morality, ethics, or religion in shaping a public policy where science plays a role. The implications of this are important for our public life and for how we order education.

Progressive politicians grew up with progressive education. Their understanding of public life, one where science is free to dictate its own terms, springs from a mistaken understanding of the place of science in a proper education. The progressive school system elevates the language of science to the exclusive language of public life while all else, the humanities, philosophy, ethics, morals, are consigned more or less to the subjective realm. Classical education must reject this ordering of public life and of educational priority. We must teach a more humble science, one mindful of science's limits and its potential for dehumanization.

In public life, the regard for science embraced by progressives can lead to dehumanizing public policy. Yuval Levin makes this point especially well in reviewing a book by Diana Degette, a progressive congresswoman from Colorado. Degette is an ardent feminist and devoted especially to the promotion of embryonic cell research. She claims that the rationale behind any public policy that touches science, regardless of the issue, be it abstinence education or stem cell research, needs to be "science-based." Levin notes, "DeGette, however, can see no way to permit other kinds of views—philosophical, ethical, moral, traditional, or religious—to influence any policy issue in which science plays a role." Any objection to science in matters of this sort is "religious" and, therefore, personal and irrelevant to public life. (Levin, 2008)

Likewise Jerome Groopman, a Harvard physician-scientist chided Leon Kass and The President's Council on Bioethics for studying Hawthorne's short story *The Birthmark* in their first meeting regarding biomedical ethics. "Using literature to warn against the scientific search for perfection is a hallmark of Kass's approach to bioethics. (Hawthorne, Homer, and Huxley are among his touchstones)." (Groopman, 2002) Homer has no relevance here? Groopman intones in closing that we should hope for "medical guidelines that are based on fact, not on literature or aesthetics—one that distinguishes real science from science fiction." (Groopman, 2002) There is no role for the humanities in ordering public life, as regards science, in Groopman's mind.

This view of science impoverishes not only our public discourse, as Degette and Groopman illustrate, but it affects even our ideas of what it is to be a human being. A recent article in *Nature*, written by educators, proposed criteria by which educators might regulate and promote their students' use of cognitive-enhancing drugs. (Greeley, 2008) Buried within the article is an assumption that there is no such thing as human agency, action which proceeds from the human as a human. People are what they are and do what they do according to their genetics and environmental conditions, not by what might spring from their souls as acting persons. For these educators, there is no such thing as motivation which springs from the human soul itself, so for them promoting self-initiative and hard work are morally equivalent means to improving a child's performance with Adderall and Ritalin might be. The progressive view of science, whether it is diminishing the ontological status of an embryo or the personal agency of a student, leads to dehumanization.

Classical educators come from a richer milieu than progressives. This type of dichotomy of the sciences and the humanities will not stand for us. Classical education understands that there are timeless and objective elements of ethics and virtue, that the beautiful in art and literature is not simply a matter of convention, that the integrity of philosophy and metaphysics still holds, and that there is the possibility of a reasoned faith. These are all features of classical education that are at odds with the scientific materialism which informs much of our public life. To assert this program, we must teach a more humble science, one consistent with classical ends for education.

The sources for a more humble science come from a consideration of the philosophical roots of science, as well as the limits science has itself discovered, especially those from the twentieth century. Philip Overby notes, "The original defense of natural science, by men like Descartes and Spinoza, was not so much a refutation as a quiet beheading of preceding philosophies. That is, modern science refutes metaphysical questions not by addressing them but by ignoring them." (Oberby, 2005) The philosophical progenitors of science began specifically by laying aside metaphysics. This was in part a revolt against Aristotle and his comprehensive influence over the medieval period, but it was also a commitment that by putting away these considerations, knowledge more useful to the relief of man's estate might be developed. They limited their consideration of the world to matter (material causes) and tangible things acting on matter (efficient causes).

While it is true that considering the world only from the standpoint of material and efficient causes has been successful technologically, there have been losses along the way. In the modern world, we cannot talk about purposes in nature. Considerations of purpose are now completely outside of the bounds of science. Much of the resistance to Intelligent Design theory comes from the idea that purpose itself is an idea antithetical to science. The idea of the existence of human nature at all is a casualty of this mindset as well.

We are also hampered in our exploration of origins. John Lennox (Lennox, 2007) notes that given the assumptions of modern science regarding the nature of causation, something like evolution was bound to be accepted as an explanation of our origins. In a perspective where material and efficient causation is all that exists, there was no other possible conclusion. The exclusion of purpose from biology invites evolution as an explanation and makes it the only possible solution to the question of our origin.

Colin Gunton points out that one of the effects of modern philosophy, which has grown up with and in response to modern science, has been to alienate modern people from the creation that they inhabit. Idealistic philosophy, such as that of Kant, radically separates the subjective from the objective. The moral and natural are separated as well. An extended quote is illustrative:

> Kant's view of the mind's assertive activity generates what can only be called a technocratic attitude to the world around us, encouraging attitudes of dominance and disparaging receptivity. Despite the astonishing success of modern science in understanding the world... there

is at another level a serious crisis in human life. The personal and physical universes we inhabit have been so divorced that the morality we should adopt to our world is a matter of scandal and confusion. Understanding is so divorced from questions of our being and that of the world that we see a mindless rape of nature in the interests of short-term human gain. This divorce of the natural and the moral universe is perhaps the worst legacy of the Enlightenment, and the most urgent challenge facing modern humankind. (Gunton, 1985)

Consideration of the shortcomings of the philosophy that informs modern science is one way to encourage a more humble science. The results that modern philosophy and science have given us are not unalloyed goods. The alienation that Gunton describes is real. Humility in the application of science is a necessity for our humanity's sake. There are also developments in modern physics and mathematics themselves that engender more humility in science.

In the early part of the nineteenth century, the great physicist LaPlace proposed a paradigm for physics. According to him, if there was a sufficient intelligence that could conceive of and simultaneously measure the velocities and positions of all particles in the universe, then that intelligence could understand not only the present state of things but all of history and the future. LaPlace conceived a way that the entire universe might be understood. This might be a grand project for physics to explain the universe in terms of mechanical causes. Not just physics, but chemistry and biology would be explainable in mathematical and physical terms.

Twentieth century physics has refuted this hope. The Heisenberg uncertainty principle states that the simultaneous knowledge of the exact position and velocity of any particle is not possible. This principle comes out of experimental science but has vast implications for the mechanicity of scientific explanation of the universe. This principle is not simply an *epistemological truth*, a reflection of how much we may know, but it is an *ontological truth*, a statement of how things are in the universe. A type of freedom or contingency is built into the cosmos that escapes mechanistic certainty. While much of the certainty we observe comes back to us through statistics, the iron lock of mechanistic physics is broken. A more humble notion of knowability, and thus technical control, is encouraged.

Another source of scientific humility comes from mathematics. In the early part of the twentieth century Russell and Whitehead published the *Principia Mathematica*. This work attempts to reduce all mathematics and mathematical truths into a well-defined set of axioms and inference rules in symbolic logic. For our purposes it represents a type of reductionism akin to the type that Laplace might have envisioned. Mathematics, according to Lennox, "might be reduced to a set of written marks that could be manipulated according to prescribed rules without any attention being paid to the applications that would give 'significance' to those marks." (Lennox, 2007) This was the so called *Entscheidungsproblem*. Solving this problem positively would have great implications for scientific reductionism generally.

In 1931, the Austrian mathematician Kurt Gdel published a paper entitled "On the Formally Undecidable Propositions of Principia Mathematica and Related Systems." This paper and a subsequent one established Gdel's First and Second Incompleteness Theorems. Gdel actually proved that a positive solution to the *Entscheidungsproblem* was impossible. He "demonstrated that the arithmetic with which we are all familiar is incomplete: that is, in any system that has a finite set of axioms and rules of inference and which is large enough to contain ordinary arithmetic, there are always true statements of the system that cannot be proved on the basis of that set of axioms and those rules of inference." In a sense, in any mathematical system, some elements need to be assumed, taken by faith. As Lennox points out, "...mathematics is the only religion that can prove that it is a religion!" (Lennox, 2007) This is a great blow to scientific reductionism coming out of science itself.

There are sources for humility in science gained from a consideration of the philosophical roots and shortcomings of modern science to deal with matters of purpose. Further, modern philosophy which attempts to account for modern science has alienating qualities that fail to promote wholeness in life, and this should cause us to question the comprehensiveness of scientific claims. Also, modern science has uncovered shortcomings that limit the mechanistic aspirations of science and the reductionist tendencies of science.

Transferring these insights to the pedagogical realm will be difficult. The present ascendancy of the progressive movement in the United States politically attests to the durability of that notion in modern life. Technology and progress are difficult to disparage since our lives are organized so thoroughly around them both. The program to teach a more humble science must itself begin humbly. When we teach physics, we must explain in a rudimentary way what philosophical assumptions are behind science. We must point out also, at the appropriate time in a child's education, the shortcomings of modern science in explaining human life and in ordering our public life.

---

Dr. Ross Betts, physician, husband of Lynn, and father of four, developed an interest in classical Lutheran education through homeschooling. Dr. Betts serves as President of the American Friends of Augustine College, a small liberal arts college in Ottawa, Canada.

## Teaching English

*by Erika Mildred*

### Introduction

Those who teach within English departments today, whether on the elementary, secondary, or post-secondary level, know the important and sometimes cumbersome set of responsibilities that fall upon them as they prepare children to be effective readers, writers, thinkers, and communicators. Western Civilization courses expose our children to a myriad of great works throughout the course of history, but obviously there are far more significant works to cover than class time can offer, and the remaining pieces of literary greatness are often thrust to the English teacher. In addition to literature, English classes at all levels consist, or at least should consist, of studies of the English language at the grammatical and logical levels, usage of the English language through written composition, and rhetorical expression of the English language through oral argumentation and creative demonstration.

Most if not all teachers of English have felt the pressure of properly dividing the time and focus of a modern student's study within the English classroom. Understandably, some well-intentioned instructors have focused primarily on one aspect of the total English curriculum to the neglect of one or more of the other components. We often see this neglect most vividly in the study of grammar. Rationalizing this imperative study away, teachers may think that students will learn grammatical rules for great writing simply by reading great literature or that students find grammatical studies so tedious and mundane that meaningful application becomes futile. Modern grammar studies with a classical approach, such as *The Shurley Method* grammar series, have helped greatly to elevate the study of grammar back into a proper level of significance within the English classroom, but in reality, this just fixes a symptom.

At the crux of the cause is the need for a change of mindset among English teachers. The truth of the matter is that our students *must* study grammar, literature, writing, speaking, and critical thinking within the walls of the English classroom. They *must* know how to express themselves effectively at all levels of the *Trivium*. They *must* learn from the great communicators of the past and through cultivation develop their own creative voice. And, in addition to these necessities, they *must* learn to develop these communicative requisites through various technological media in addition to the more traditional avenues of pen and paper. Needless to say, an effective English course will perfectly blend the writings and musings of the great thinkers of the past with the cultivating of great writers, speakers, and thinkers of new generations. Few if any would argue that these expectations are not mandatory. The question then is one of pragmatics and can be encompassed by a single word: how? The answer is horizontal integration within the English classroom.

Horizontal integration requires a teacher to intentionally connect literature, grammar, composition, and discourse to one another and to help students of English to do the same. Following are several methods to achieve horizontal integration.

### Comprehensive Grammatical Instruction

Grammar is the language of language; one cannot begin to talk about how we communicate without knowing and understanding the rules upon which that communication is built. No one can truly appreciate Chaucer, Shakespeare, Mark Twain, or Robert Frost without understanding what rules they were purposely, defiantly, proudly breaking for a specific effect. Further, we cannot expect our students to reach future rhetorical greatness without first having grammatical mastery. We must be prescriptive in our instruction, and we must incorporate grammar into every part of our English curriculum. Studying grammar for its own sake is good, but it is not enough. We must also encourage our students to look at the grammar of the pieces of literature they are reading or to listen for the effect of grammar in the orations they are studying. We must have them perform revisions on every written composition, and we must correct their grammatical errors in such a way that they recognize and learn from their mistakes. In this way, we lay a strong foundation upon which more complex, profound communication is built.

## Rhetorical Devices

One of the easiest and most effective ways to horizontally integrate in the English classroom is to teach students several dozen rhetorical devices. Starting at the grammar level with the memorization of the names and definitions of devices along with examples from composition and forensics and moving to the dialectic and rhetoric stages by having students use these devices in their own writing, English teachers can provide students with an arsenal of superior words and phrases for both written and oral communication. Moreover, after studying these devices and how they work most effectively, students can analyze literature and speeches, learning from the masters and developing an aesthetic, rhetorical appreciation for their works.

A wide spectrum of rhetorical devices should be taught including balance (such as parallelism, chiasmus, and antithesis), restatement (such as epanalepsis, epistrophe, and anaphora), drama (such as anacoluthon, apophasis, and rhetorical question), emphasis (such as hyperbole, litotes, and polysyndeton), syntax (such as zeugma, anastrophe, and appositives), figurative language (such as epithet, simile, catechresis, and apostrophe), sound and word play (such as alliteration, onomatopoeia, and irony), and clarity and transition (such as exemplum, amplification, and metabasis). These devices have been used by great communicators for centuries, and having a knowledge and mastery of these will not only equip your students to become better writers but also will provide a connective bridge between the various topics of study found in English curricula.

## Modeling

While reading the greatest thinkers throughout Western history should be centered on discovering what is true, noble, and beautiful, students of English can also use these same pieces of literary achievement as essays, short stories, and poetry from which to copy the various styles and techniques. Modeling can work equally well with the orations of Cicero, Abraham Lincoln, Winston Churchill, and others. Modeling is not a new concept in education; it belongs in every Classical school, as it has been used as a learning tool in the schools of Socrates and Aristotle. In order to copy a style, one must first study and analyze it. Again, knowing the rules of grammar and ample rhetorical devices will allow students to recognize the brilliant communicative elements that have allowed these pieces of literature and oratory to withstand the test of time. Students will also discover that modeling is not only something their English teacher encourages them to do; it is also something that other literary greats, such as Chaucer and Shakespeare, have done for centuries before. After all, it has been said that imitation is the most sincere form of flattery.

## Literary Analysis

Finally, writing and speaking about literature are a key components for horizontal integration in English classes. Teachers can have students do in-depth character analyses, cause and effect papers, line-by-line interpretations of poetry, research papers, oral argumentation, and the like, all aimed at connecting the written and spoken word together with literature. As students write and speak about what they read, they begin to recognize the ongoing Great Conversation of Western Civilization. More importantly, they begin to *participate* in the conversation. Thus, they can see their written and oral communicative works as extending beyond the assignment itself.

## Conclusion

In the modern English classroom, teachers, especially those in a classical setting, must design a comprehensive curriculum using strategies and techniques that provide horizontal integration. The integration must be intentional and thorough, and when students are at a cognitively appropriate level, the students must be made aware of the integration. After all, at the end of formal schooling, each student indeed is a single being, not truncated or parsed into communicative components, but presented to the world as a singular whole and judged based on the totality of his communicative effectiveness.

---

Erika Mildred, writer and speaker for the Consortium for Classical Lutheran Education, has taught mathematics, English, Logic, and Rhetoric in classical high schools; assisted with classical curriculum development, and provided private tutoring. Erika currently tutors from home where she cares for her two young children, Emma and Jordan.

Notes

## The Progymnasmata

*by Rev. Stephen Kieser*

A Roman education consisted of the acquisition of the most basic language skills - especially reading and writing - and a period of exercises with the teacher of grammar (grammaticus). When the boy was ready, training would continue under a teacher of rhetoric (rhetor). Special emphasis was placed on the boy's readiness. No one was to be passed on to the rhetor before he was deemed well prepared. This kind of education was insistent that *students* were to be taught, not *subjects*. (Murphy, 1990, p. 40)

Marcus Fabius Quintilian wrote of an educational system with the purpose of *facilitas*, that is, the capacity to produce appropriate and effective language in any situation. His method for accomplishing *facilitas* included five stages: Precept, Imitation, Progymnasmata, Declamation, and Sequencing. (Murphy, 1990, p. 40) Writing and rhetoric were to go hand in hand, since writing was viewed as a major means to oral eloquence. (Murphy, 1990, p. 19) Quintilian's five stages trained the hand that would influence the tongue.

### Progymnasmata

Quite woodenly, "progymnasmata" means "before naked." In the sports arena, the gymnasium was the place where one went nude in participation of athletic events. (Spivey and Squire, 2004, p. 27) In the rhetorical progymnasmata, the language of physical education was applied to intellectual studies. (Bonner, 1977, p. 250) These were academic exercises, preliminary and necessary before receiving instruction from a rhetor where the student would begin his official studies in prose. Under the grammaticus the student would study the basics of language and literature; however, little to no prose was undertaken. This was left for the rhetor. Boys usually began progymnasmata sometime between the ages of 12 and 15. (Bonner, 1977, p. 250) Progymnasmata was preliminary in the sense that they would lead the student to full-scale mock deliberative and mock legal speeches known as *hypothese* by the Greeks and *suasoriae* and *controversiae* by the Romans.

Some of the exercises (i.e. Thesis) date back to classical Greece and a standard set of exercises developed during the Hellenistic Age. During these 300 years, Greek culture dominated most of the eastern Mediterranean and the Middle East. The exercises were fairly complete by the first century BC. Four Greek treatises, or textbooks, were written on progymnasmata during the time of the Roman Empire and studied throughout the Byzantine period. They are written by or are attributed to Theon, Hermogenes, Aphthonius, and Nicolaus. The only Latin account was Quintilian's "Training on Oratory." (94 AD)

### The Exercises: A General Overview

The easiest exercises were at the beginning of the course, as one would expect: The Instructive Saying (chreia), the Maxim (sententia), the Fable (apologus, fable, and mythos) and the mythological Narrative (narration), each of these will be examined more closely in the next section of this article. In previous grammar, many sayings and stories had been written and rewritten via drills in copying and dictation so that they were known by heart. The first of the progymnasmata challenged student to reproduce these in their own words, explain, and expand them into short essays. The grammaticus or rhetor focused on the individual student and employed half a dozen methods in each exercise. The instructor was never satisfied with mere explanations and expansions, but regarded the boy successful when he proceeded to a confirmation and refutation of the saying, fable or narrative and argued that it was sound and plausible, or the reverse. (Bonner, 1977, p. 253)

After these initial exercises, the oratory exercise became more practical. Boys developed Commonplaces, themes involving Praise and Denunciation; and Comparisons, all of which involved amplification. These were then followed by exercises which demanded a student's imagination as well as a range of expression. The speech in character was a favorite. The student impersonated some well-known character in myth or history and was to speak as the character might have spoken in some dire crisis or dilemma. Next was the full-scale Description. This proved to be a valuable asset to an orator keen on showmanship. Finally, the student was to argue a case both pro and con, in the Thesis and Discussion of a Law. Having completed these preliminary writing exercises, the student was ready for the *suasoria* and *controversia* in Declamation. (Bonner, 1977, p. 253)

The order of the parts of the progymnasmata was not adhered to strictly, but was adapted somewhat as the grammaticus or rhetor thought would be best for each student. Two important notes must be made. First, although the exercises were to be written, they were to be expressed orally. Writing was a means toward rhetoric. Second, while the exercises were directed toward oratorical excellence, they were also regarded as the foundation for a wider sphere of literary activity, and they exerted a considerable influence on the methods of composition for both prose writers and poets. In each exercise, the fodder was the classical authors of antiquity. Students were expected to know them well. (Bonner, 1977, p. 253)

**A Closer Look**

**Fables:**

Often Aesop was used. For younger students, Aesop Fables were amusing and enjoyable to learn. First, the student orally retold the story. Then the story would be written down, and it was to be more than a simple verbatim recitation of the fable. The fable was to be expanded, with details developed. The writer, for example, was encouraged to have animals give short speeches in keeping with the story line and characters, not to depart in a new or different direction. Because Fables taught a moral lesson, teachers emphasized it. Sometimes the student was given a Fable and then asked to determine what the moral lesson was. Other times, the student was asked to illustrate a Fable from a historical occurrence. While paraphrase was not listed as a separate exercise, paraphrased retelling played a primary role in every exercise. (Bonner, 1977, p. 255)

**Anecdote or The Saying:**

These exercises focused on a useful Saying (chreia), for example: Isocrates said that the root of education is bitter, its fruit sweet. One of the drills used with Anecdote was to have students "decline" the saying by placing the subject in different cases. For example:

Nominative—Isocrates said, . . .

Genitive—There is a story of Isocrates having said. . .

Dative—It occurred to Isocrates to remark. . .

Accusative—They say that Isocrates observed. . .

Vocative—You once said, Isocrates. . .

Another exercise of Anecdote was to paraphrase a saying, provide an explanation to show how it was true, give an example, and finally after a quotation from the poets that supported the saying and reinforced the argument's truthfulness. (Bonner, 1977, p. 259)

**Narration:**

Boys were given narrative themes which were closely related to their own studies. The simplest form was myth. Rhetorical embellishment was not expected, but each student should become very familiar with the subject matter of each myth. In Greek, it was not uncommon for the rhetor to be involved in these exercises. Most teachers expected that their students would write in a manner that was clear, succinct, and convincing – traditional virtues of the narrative style.

Another form of Narration was the historical narrative. For this exercise, Quintilian insisted that the rhetor take over, which followed the practice that the reading of historians began at the rhetoric school. The narrative was to record strictly the events that actually occurred. The boy was to become completely familiar with the narrative, and he was to retell it orally before writing it out. The teacher would then require the boy to retell the story from different starting points, beginning in the middle or at some other point, while finding a way to include all the events of the story. It was a test of the memory and proved whether or not the students had a grasp on the historical event. When writing or speaking, care was to be taken to avoid the use of poetic, archaic, or unfamiliar words, and especially phrases that could be ambiguous. (Bonner, 1977, p. 262)

**Refutation and Confirmation:**

The writer had to examine a given story from the point of view of its general credibility and then write an essay either arguing that it was lacking likelihood, or supporting it as quite feasible. The material used was poetry. Guidelines were laid down for procedure: after setting out the alleged facts, the student was to determine whether to substantiate or refute; and whether the account was clear or obscure, possible or impossible, seemly or unseemly, consistent or inconsistent, expedient or inexpedient. His argument was to include the person, the act, the place, time, manner, and motive. (Bonner, 1977, p. 263)

## Commonplace:

This exercise was a form of amplification that could prove extremely effective in court. Commonplace was an exposure, both reasoned and emotional, of various types of evil-doers. It also had its converse, dilation, the merits and services of various types of benefactors. All kinds of vice were denounced. Cicero mentions commonplaces against an embezzler and a traitor. Quintilian instances commonplaces against an adulterer and a gambler. Other exercises were directed against a tyrant, a murderer, a traitor, and a temple-robber. The Commonplace was very similar to that of an advocate's speech in court, the main difference being that no specific individual was attacked or defended. (Bonner, 1977, p. 264)

## Enconium and Denunciation:

Closely tied to Commonplace, some also placed Enconium before Commonplace. These exercises were concerned with either praise or blame, and they dealt specifically with historical or legendary persons. Just as Commonplace had a direct use in court speeches, so also did Enconium and Denunciation have practical use in actual speeches. A major difference was that while a Commonplace might be inserted as a section of a speech, Enconium and Denunciation could take up an entire oration.

In these preliminary exercises in the rhetorical schools, attention was given to topics to be used when praising famous men or denouncing evils doers. The subjects were drawn from Greek and Roman history, though in Greek schools the praise or censure of Homeric heroes was also favored.

The method included a threefold division of a person's praiseworthy feature, classified as either physical properties, qualities of the mind and character, or extraneous accessions, whether inherited or acquired. Students were to write chronologically, considering first the origin and background of the person concerned. If of noble birth, he might be praised as having matched or surpassed the glory of his ancestors. If of humble origin, he might be praised for having risen in the world from a lowly beginning. His country was to be introduced as well. Any particular manifestations connected with his birth (e.g., an omen or prophecy) should be included. Next, extraneous circumstances were recorded—resources that he acquired such as wealth, power, influence, and friendships; and how these contributed to the reason for praise. After this, a closer look at the man himself. Perhaps his physical attributes (stature, vigor, handsomeness), but even more his quality of mind and character. Stress was to be given to attributes that were beneficial to the community, rather than to his own well-being. Finally, praise or censure was made based on his actions in his career. (Bonner, 1977, p. 265)

## Comparison:

This required students to make a balanced assessment by being given a pair of individuals whose merits or demerits appeared to have similarity. The object was to prove one superior over the other. The more evenly balanced the two beings compared, the more care and judgment required. (Bonner, 1977, p. 267)

## Speech in Character or Impersonation:

So far, students would have learned a great deal about actual discourse, but they would not have been put in the position of a person making a speech. This exercise was a solid step in that direction. Here it was necessary for the student to imagine himself in the position of a historical or mythological person or creature who is at some critical point in life, and to attempt to speak as that person might have spoken in those circumstances. The style had to be appropriate to the speaker's character, time of life, status, and to the particular circumstances. (Bonner, 1977, p. 268)

## Description:

This exercise had wide applicability. The student was to describe a place such as a meadow, harbor, island, seashore; a season such as spring or summer; an occasion, such as a festive gathering; a happening, such as a storm, famine, plague, or earthquake; a war scene, such as a land or sea battle; or a description of a person, animal, or activity such as the making of a shield or laying of fortifications The writer was to describe the topic in a clear and graphic manner. It was to be written in such a way that you could see what was being described. If kept within reason, it was a means by which to encourage imagination and observation, and to develop the power of expression. (Bonner, 1977, p. 270)

## Thesis and Discussion of a Law:

These were considered of particular importance, because they developed the student's ability to argue both sides of a debatable question. In earlier exercises, the student had learned the art of arguing both ways in limited scope, such as that of legends. Now the field widened, and additional topics were tackled. Themes included: Should one marry or not? Should one have children or not? Should one take to seafaring or not? Should a wise man engage in politics or not? Topics could take on a comparative form, such as: Is country life or town life preferable? Does the soldier deserve more credit than the lawyer?

When these exercises were combined with a short poem and an epilogue, they came very close to becoming a fully developed speech. The topics were generally of two types: those that dealt with daily life, such as whether or not to marry, and others that were purely speculative, such as, "Do the gods care for humanity?" (Bonner, 1977, p. 271)

## Praise and Denunciation of Laws:

The last and most advanced of the progymnasmata, this exercise involved the selection of a law—an imaginative law, an existing law, or a piece of new legislation. The student discussed the law's merits and demerits by taking the position of one who offered reasoned advice on the subject. First, the student was to examine for possible obscurity (use of ambiguous words, synonymous words that might create confusion, syntactical ambiguity, or inadequate definitions). After review of the wording, the student was to show whether the law contained any conflict within itself, and whether the stipulation of the law should be limited to certain persons. Then the more important issues were stated. Was the law honorable? Just? Expedient? Practical? Necessary? Upon leaving the Progymnasmata, the student would endeavor to produce an even more detailed critique of laws in the Declamation Exercises. (Bonner, 1977, p. 271)

**Conclusion:**

Progymnasmata, a series of writing exercises for the purpose of developing eloquent writers and speakers, was developed during the Greco-Roman period. Fully in use by the first centuries of the years of our Lord, these application and methods were the foundation of the education of boys and, later, also girls. The Progymnasmata instructed students in both written and oratory expression. They have stood the test of time as part and parcel to a classical education. For this reason alone, they at least deserve our attention and perhaps our consideration for a renewed and diligent use in today's classical and Lutheran classrooms.

---

The Reverend Stephen Kieser, B.A. Secondary Education from Concordia – Ann Arbor, M.A. Theology from Concordia Theological Seminary, Ft. Wayne, and M.A School Administration from Concordia – River Forest; serves as President of the Consortium for Classical and Lutheran Education. Husband to Julia and homeschooling father of seven, he and his family reside in Indiana where he serves as a Lutheran parish pastor.

## An Overview of Classical Rhetoric

*by Dr. James Tallmon*

Classical rhetoric, in its most ethical and ancient manifestation, is a way of discussing the truth with one's fellows in a manner that respects their freedom and dignity, and attempts to move them toward the Good. Of course human beings think, argue, and persuade by nature. We do these intuitively! However, there is a big difference between intuition and art. In order to master any body of knowledge as an art, one must:

1. Define it
2. Break it into parts
3. Study the parts
4. Practice

Steps 1-3 entail laying a theoretical foundation and systematically acquiring a theoretical account of the "making" process. There is no substitute for theory when one's aim is art. In *Back to the Rough Ground*, Joseph Dunne defines art (techne) as: "The kind of knowledge possessed by an expert maker; it gives him a clear conception of the why and wherefore, the how and the with what of the making process and enables him, through the capacity to offer a rational account of it, to preside over his activity with secure mastery". (Dunne, 1993, p. 9) I love the imagery of a master craftsman presiding over his art with secure mastery! There is no substitute for theory when one sets out to master an art. As has been established elsewhere, imparting such practical arts is the aim of liberal arts education.

Of liberal arts education, John Henry Cardinal Newman, in his *The Idea of a University*, writes:

> The man who has learned to think and to reason and to compare and to discriminate and to analyze, who has refined his taste, and formed his judgment, and sharpened his mental vision, will not indeed at once be a lawyer, or a pleader, or an orator, or a statesman, or a physician, or a good chemist, or a geologist, or an antiquarian, but he will be placed in that state of intellect in which he can take up any one of the sciences or callings I have referred to, or any other for which he has a taste or special talent, with an ease, a grace, a versatility, and a success, to which another is a stranger. . . . I say that a cultivated intellect, because it is a good in itself, brings with it a power and a grace to every work and occupation which it undertakes, and enables us to be more useful, and to a greater number. (Newman, 1982, pp. 124 & 6)

I appreciate these lines for a couple of reasons. First, Newman defines liberal arts education in terms of cultivating the intellect by learning to reason, forming one's judgment and sharpening one's mental vision. Second, I appreciate the way he turns the tables on the Utilitarians of his day. Newman wrote *The Idea of a University* to answer the Utilitarians' claim that university education was not very practically useful (utile). The Utilitarians were all about maximizing the greatest good to the greatest number. They felt that society would be best served by institutions of higher learning that educated in practical skills. Newman, in his erudite way, elucidates why liberal education "enables us to be more useful, and to a greater number." (Newman, 1982, pp. 151) Well said!

In order to master an art, one must first define it and then break it into its parts. I prefer to start with Aristotle's definition of rhetoric (realizing, of course, that debate over the proper definition of rhetoric predates Aristotle). Aristotle and Plato are not the only voices to speak to us of rhetoric from ancient Greece. But they are the ones featured here.

Early in his treatise on rhetoric, Aristotle defines it as: "The faculty of discovering in any given case the available means of persuasion." Many before him simply defined rhetoric as "the art of speaking." He was dissatisfied with this reductionism, so he decided, no doubt prompted by comments attributed to Socrates in *The Phaedrus*, to take a more philosophical tack in his rhetorical treatise. He realizes that his students need a theoretical understanding in order to acquire an art of rhetoric. Aristotle focuses on cultivating in his students the power to formulate lines of argument on all manner of practical questions. He identifies three arenas of such enterprise (forensic, deliberative and epideictic–that is, arguing before the bar, making one's case before the assembly, and engaging in ceremonial speaking). Much of Aristotle's *Rhetorica* is spent elucidating lines of argument useful in these three contexts. Aristotle also divides rhetoric into three constituent "modes of artistic proof": ethos, pathos and logos. Aristotle notes that, in order to persuade, the words of the speech must evoke "fellow-feeling" in the audience, the orator must put the audience in the proper frame of mind, and, of course, must give them good reasons for adopting the position being argued. Artistic proofs are those "invented" by the rhetor (i.e., orator: one who practices rhetoric); inartistic proofs are merely used. So, those artistic proofs, formed by the words of the speech itself, are most fully developed that combine good logical support with appropriate appeals to passion and are spoken so as to underscore the trustworthiness of the speaker. For an elaborated treatment of Aristotle's three modes of proof, see Rhetoric Ring, "Ethos, Pathos, and Logos". (http://www.rhetoricring.com/)

Your student will need to study the foundational concepts discussed at the Rhetoric Ring and other sites linked there that discuss Rhetorical Theory. The "RinGo exercise" at the end of Chapter One will guide you through the "Overview" and "Rhetoric in the Classical Liberal Arts." However, I think one can get bogged down with theory at a too young age, and rhetoric is, in the final analysis, a very practical enterprise. Be sure to check out the tips before you wax too philosophical with your younger pupils. Of course liberal arts learning necessitates laying a theoretical foundation, but, at ages twelve to seventeen, I recommend focusing on fun exercises in debate, speech composition, memorization, and oral interpretation, graduated to give students a "layered" learning experience. That way they experience the joy of working with the language and cultivate the ability to work with words, as their grasp of the art spirals upward. There is no substitute for theory when the aim is mastery of art, because without theory there is no framework for understanding; however, as young scholars are introduced to an art, theory should be dispensed, strategically, at appropriate learning intervals, and in concert with exercises designed to cultivate specific skills. There is time later for contemplating the deeper concerns of rhetorical theory (and believe me, there are plenty!). A too heavy concentration on matters theoretical may quench the joy of learning. If your philosophically inclined 16-year old student insists that he or she is ready to tackle rhetorical theory in earnest, see the readings at adv.htm. Back to the overview.

Two more concepts in classical rhetoric, associated normally with the Sophists, are *kairos* and *to prepon*. *Kairos* is timing. Timing is an important element of rhetoric. Consider the difficulty in getting a laugh when one muffs the punch line of a joke. Why so? For one thing, it throws off the timing. *To prepon* has to do with fitness for the occasion. One does not preach only hell-fire and brimstone in a Lutheran church. It's just not appropriate; it's not fitting. On the other hand, some of the most poignant speeches are identified as such because they were such "a fitting response to the occasion."

By the Roman era, rhetoric had been divided into five sub-arts, the Five Classical Canons of Rhetoric. They are: Invention, Disposition, Style, Memory and Delivery. For the purposes of this overview, let us think of them in terms of a practical guide to preparing a speech (realizing there is much more to them). We will return to the Five Canons later, but this initial overview constitutes a primer.

For each canon, I will phrase a question that one might ask oneself when composing a speech.

- *Invention* - "What can I say?"

  Invention has to do with the legwork; of coming up with good ideas. Invention entails doing research, (what is there to say on my topic, generally,) and narrowing the topic, or deciding one's "angle" (out of everything one could say, what do I want to say about this topic, at this time, with respect to this particular audience?)

  But why would this process be called "invention"? When one is engaged in persuasive speaking or writing, one must invent, or construct, arguments. Invention is a very involved part of the art of rhetoric. It entails much more than merely deciding one's topic, but these thoughts will suffice for the purposes of this overview. For a fuller treatment, see Rhetoric Ring.

  You've decided your angle and gathered a goodly amount of supporting evidence. Now you need to organize your thoughts.

- *Disposition* - "What arrangement will make the most sense?"

  Make an assertion, support it with evidence, reasoning, and an illustration if necessary. Make a transition and move on to your next point. One must balance elaborating points with overloading the audience. Most textbooks go on at length here regarding spatial, versus logical, versus chronological patterns of arrangement. (Chapter Two, "On Disposition," discusses more fully strategies of arrangement.) I generally just teach Plato's "Clever Butcher" analogy:

  Plato said that a clumsy butcher takes a chicken and hacks it all to pieces making a mess of the whole thing. A clever butcher, on the other hand, realizes that the chicken has natural divisions, called joints, and uses those to cleanly divide the chicken. So, when organizing a speech, I just tell my students to look for the natural divisions of the topic and organize it around those. If during practice the speech doesn't seem to flow properly, all they have to do is reorganize. It does not need to be any more complicated than that.

  One thing is certain. When one builds a beautiful edifice and takes a trip to the emporium to buy materials, one does not just wheel one's cart down the aisle and grab materials willy-nilly. One buys the tools and materials needed according to the blue print. Disposition is about establishing a blueprint which guides the "making process."

  As with building a fine edifice, style is the key to introducing to the enterprise an element of beauty. Visit the "Speech Builder's Emporium; see the"Edifice Metaphor."

- *Style* - "Where is emphasis needed?"

  Most people don't envision a shanty when they think of their dream home. When it comes to speeches and papers, aesthetics are important. This is so for a couple of reasons. First, in order to move an audience, one ought to evoke as vivid a mental image as possible. This is where pathos and style come together. Second, beautiful speeches inspire. Learning to use language artfully, to appeal not only to the mind but also to the imagination and the heart, is a very humanizing activity for both speaker and audience. Images give impact.

- *Memory* - "How can I remember the points in order to make the speech flow?"

  Memory is not memorization. This canon has more to do with mnemonic devices. Back when orators had to deliver large amounts of text from memory, they invested some time in constructing means of committing to memory main points, to foster fluidity.

- *Delivery* - "Given this situation, how might I most effectively deliver this message?"

  Delivery may be subdivided into the physical and the vocal. Physical aspects of delivery are: posture, eye contact, movement and gestures. Vocal aspects have to do with tone, rate, pitch, volume and so on. Memory and delivery are rather obvious and were, for much of history, considered the "lost canons of rhetoric."

These are the Five Classical Canons of Rhetoric. In order to master an art, one needs to define it, break it into parts, study the parts and then practice it until it becomes second nature. This brief sketch can give you a beginning. The journey continues by following and studying the RhetoricRing.com, composing and delivering speeches and papers, engaging in a few organized debates, composing some orations and oral interpretation pieces, and learning to think quickly on one's feet. You may find of interest the PowerPoint presentation posted on the "Rhetoric in the Liberal Arts" page of the Rhetoric Ring. One could benefit from watching the slides while reading the text of Chapter One above, because it is, for all practical purposes, the narrative that constitutes much of that presentation.

As one acquires an art of rhetoric, one will also hone one's ability to engage in practical reasoning. That is why dialectic and rhetoric are closely linked. This is also why debate or argumentation, speech, and public speaking go hand-in-hand. One must, therefore, define practical reasoning and break it into its constituent parts as well. Having done so, our overview of rhetoric will be complete.

I define practical reasoning as:

Cultivating the intellectual abilities to:

- Identify and evaluate assumptions
- Follow an argument to its conclusion
- Spot contradictions and faulty logic
- Draw appropriate distinctions.
- Avoid extremes
- Exercise foresight

All of the fundamental tools outlined here, dispensed in dialectic and rhetoric, equip one to deal effectively with ideas. They equip students to reason systematically, identify and evaluate assumptions, spot contradictions and faulty logic, and think with quick precision.

For Further reading consider:

*Wisdom and Eloquence: a Christian Paradigm For Classical Learning* (2006) Robert Littlejohn and Charles T. Evans. Crossway Books: Wheaton, IL.

---

Dr. James Tallmon, B.S. and M.A. in Speech Communication, PhD in Rhetoric and Ethics, has served as writer, speaker, and previous Board member for the Consortium for Classical and Lutheran Education. Formerly the Professor of Rhetoric and Director of Debate at Patrick Henry College, Dr. Tallmon serves as Headmaster and Teacher at Trinity Lutheran School in Cheyenne, Wyoming.

Notes

## The Logic and Purpose of History

*by Heather Judd*

*What is history? How should we teach it? Why should we teach it?* These questions are interrelated, and we can only teach history effectively once we have answers to each of them.

### Defining History

First, what is history? The simplest definition might be something like: "History is the study of events that happened in the past." Of course, "events that happened in the past" could apply just as well to the buttering of one's morning toast as to Hannibal's crossing of the Alps. Thus history is properly limited to the study of significant events in the past.

Since it is based on a factual record of events, history stands on a belief in objective truth that can be separated from falsehood. Nevertheless, many modern historians delight in emphasizing a relativistic approach to history. The statement "Christopher Columbus discovered the New World in 1492" is called into question in every aspect: "Discovered?" According to whose standards? Native peoples lived there before he arrived. "New World?" New to whom? "Christopher Columbus?" An Anglicization of the Italian *Christofori Columbo.* "1492?" Whose calendar is being used? Why is it better than another? The postmodern teacher erodes truth and establishes a framework for existential uncertainty in all things. Oscar Handlin, a former Harvard history professor, comments on this phenomenon in his book *Truth in History*:

> . . . not a few [scholars] followed the deceptive path from acknowledgment that no person was entirely free of prejudice or capable of attaining a totally objective view of the past to the conclusion that all efforts to do so were vain and that, in the end, the past was entirely a recreation emanating from the mind of the historian (Handlin, 1979, p. 410).

By denying truth in history, we open ourselves to the possibility that we are all simply madmen, and that history and myth are indistinguishable.

History, although not one of the original seven liberal arts, has existed as a discipline at least since the time of Herodotus, more than four hundred years before Christ. In our current incarnation of classical education, it often serves as a convenient discipline around which to orient the curriculum, but history is far more than a hub into which we may conveniently stick our other disciplinary spokes. Teaching history—and Western Civilization in particular—is decidedly a purging of progressivism. The progressive field of social studies encourages teaching about communities, social skills, racism, feminism, and tolerance. The time period makes little difference. The United States of the 1960's would serve just as well as the Golden Age of ancient Athens. By cherry-picking historical events to examine social problems, social studies promotes a relativistic view that denies that some men or civilizations were greater than others. Still, the reality remains: Either Rome defeated Carthage or she did not. History demands a belief in objective truth.

### How to Teach History: The Early Years

How, then, should we teach the objective truths of history to our students? Dates and names, events and places are the individual links in the chronological chain of history, and in the early years history should give students the most pertinent and complete set of "links" possible. Students may begin in these years to connect individual pieces of information, but that is not yet the primary goal.

Historical dates are the simplest of the links that grammar students will learn, as they are short, contained, and objective. To this end, each teacher needs to derive some list of historical events with key dates for students to internalize. Preexisting lists are convenient, but they require critical evaluation since they often reflect an objectionable philosophical or theological bias. To complement the learning of key dates, a visual timeline, prominently displayed and frequently referenced, helps students think chronologically not only about history, but also about literature, science, and other studies.

Along with dates, names, and events, the young student should learn certain historical causes and effects, but he should not be expected to extrapolate them himself. Rather, the teacher should explain, model, or actually do such linking for him. This information can then marinate in the student's mind until he again confronts these historical issues on a higher level. The reasoning in which he will later engage can only derive new knowledge by forming connections between knowledge already possessed; thus, a student who lacks this early training will struggle later to compensate for his historical missing links.

## How to Teach History: The Middle Years

With the piecemeal approach of progressive education, students are hard-pressed to "progress" to a mature, analytical understanding of history. A classical approach strives in the middle years to join the links of chronology through an apprenticeship of modeling and imitation by which students move from seeing the logical connections made by others to drawing connections from given information, and finally to identifying and connecting facts on their own. If successfully imbued, this process is one which will guide students in every area of study and make history breathe with a new life of its own.

This deductive process begins with generalizations. In history, this means students should understand what the traditional eras of Western Civilization are, and why they are so divided. Students should be able to characterize Ancient History, the Middle Ages, and the Modern Era and test their characterizations against events within each one. The three major historical classifications are not random, and students should grasp the essential differences among them, furthering their understanding through sub-eras such as the Greek Archaic Age, the High Middle Ages, or the Industrial Revolution.

With this framework in place, students can begin the reasoning that will help them link historical events into a causal chain. Though the timeline of history is without deviation, the connections between its events are complex, resulting in a chain rich with intricately intertwining loops, twists, and filaments. Central to historical studies in these middle years is the shift from "what" to "why." As students gain practice in assessing causal relationships, they can become increasingly confident and independent in their conclusions.

Another form of question that hones logical skills is comparison and contrast. The process is simple, but the findings can be profound. By this practice students discover historical patterns that can help them more deftly form the links between other ideas, even while reviewing what they have already learned. When studying Nebuchadnezzar's Neo-Babylonian Empire, students could compare it to Hammurabi's Old Babylonian Empire. Or they might contrast Marc Antony with Octavian and speculate whether Actium would have ended differently had each man possessed different strengths or weaknesses. Or they might weigh the French and American Revolutions. By asking what makes these things similar and what distinguishes them, students also sharpen their skill at defining terms and grasping essential characteristics, which will ultimately help them create a broad and well-defined concept of history.

The use of primary sources provides further opportunity for critical thinking. Students in their middle years of school should understand the difference between primary and secondary sources and begin to use primary sources in their historical studies. To avoid having this practice become a prolonged and painful comprehension exercise that ends with little historical insight, it is often best to incorporate primary sources in small, edited, annotated doses that allow students to grasp the main point with ease.

Finally, historical analysis should expand to incorporate other disciplines such as philosophy, literature, science, arts, and religion. How did the rise of Christianity alter the Roman Empire and contribute to its transition into the Middle Ages? In what ways did the Renaissance become a rebirth of old ideas from the Greeks and Romans? How is the Scientific Revolution related to the Enlightenment era and the modern world? Look at artwork from these time periods. Listen to the music. Through such complex connections, students will begin the lifelong task of understanding the world, its people, and their thoughts.

## Why to Teach History: An Overarching View

These pedagogical practicalities still leave this fundamental question open: Why teach history?

First of all, history is a story in which we are both readers and participants. We should be curious about the nature of this story and the end toward which it presses. However, if history is only narrative, there is little to distinguish it from literature, and its basis on truth seems no longer essential. Furthermore, merely narrating history without considering its causes and implications is impossible in practicality, for we as human beings are compelled to search for some greater meaning in the stories we read, hear, and recite. On this topic, one contemporary historian reflects:

> The problem of causation, the most vexatious facing the historian, is beyond complete 'solution'—that is, to the permanent satisfaction of all manners of men. It bristles with philosophical and practical difficulties. Are human events 'determined,' or can individuals choose paths to follow?
>
> . . . Should we therefore abandon efforts to find causes? Some historians do, preferring to deal in non-causal explanations. But to abandon the search for causes would be other than human (that is, it is not likely to happen), and it would leave us with formless and meaningless historical literature (Shafer, 1975, p. 52).

History urges us to ask, "What does this mean for us and for the future?" Historians of every era have agreed that history has a didactic purpose. The Father of History, Herodotus, lays out his didactic intentions in the preface to his history:

> This is the showing forth of the inquiry of Herodotus of Halicarnassos, to the end that neither the deeds of men may be forgotten by lapse of time, nor the works great and marvelous, which have been produced some by Hellenes and some by Barbarians, may lose their renown; and

especially that the causes may be remembered for which these waged war with one another. (Herodotus, 1890, preface) [3]

Eleven centuries and four thousand miles distant from Herodotus, the medieval historian Bede similarly expresses a didactic purpose for his *Ecclesiastical History of the English People*:

> To the most glorious King Ceolwulf, Bede, servant of Christ and priest. . . . I gladly acknowledge the unfeigned enthusiasm with which, not content merely to lend an attentive ear to hear the words of Holy Scripture, you devote yourself to learn the sayings and doings of the men of old, and more especially the famous men of our own race. Should history tell of good men and their good estate, the thoughtful listener is spurred on to imitate the good; should it record the evil ends of wicked men, no less effectually the devout and earnest listener or reader is kindled to eschew what is harmful and perverse, and himself with greater care pursue those things which he has learned to be good and pleasing in the sight of God. This you perceive, clear-sighted as you are; and therefore, in you zeal for the spiritual well-being of us all, you wish to see my History more widely known, for the instruction of yourself and those over whom divine authority has appointed you to rule (Bede, 1999, p. 3).

Likewise, early in the Modern Age Sir Walter Raleigh expounds at length in his preface to The History of the World on the didactic nature and use of history:

> By [history] (I say) it is, that we live in the very time when [the world] was created: we behold how it was governed: how it was covered with waters, and again repeopled: how kings and kingdoms have flourished and fallen, and for what virtue and piety God made prosperous; and for what vice and deformity he made wretched, both the one and the other. . . . In a word, we may gather out of history a policy no less wise than eternal; by the comparison and application of other men's fore-passed miseries with our own like errors and ill deservings (Raleigh, 1938, pp. 69-70).

Even more pertinent to developing a particularly Lutheran rationale for teaching history is Martin Luther's preface to a history written by his contemporary Galeatius Capella. Luther begins:

> Histories are . . . a very precious thing. For what the philosophers, wise men, and all men of reason can teach or devise which can be useful for an honorable life, that the histories present powerfully with examples and happenings making them visually so real, as though one were there and saw everything happen that the word had previously conveyed to the ears by mere teaching* (Luther, 1960, p. 275).

---

[3]accessed through "Project Gutenberg" June 2007 http://www.gutenberg.org/dirs/etext01/1hofh10.txt

Thus far, Luther acknowledges the power of history's narrative appeal, but he goes on:

> There one finds both how those who were pious and wise acted, refrained from acting, and lived, how they fared and how they were rewarded, as well as how those who were wicked and foolish lived and how they were repaid for it. Upon thorough reflection one finds that almost all laws, art, good counsel, warning, threatening, terrifying, comforting, strengthening, instruction, prudence, wisdom, discretion, and all virtues well up out of the narratives and histories as from a living fountain (Luther, 1960, p. 275).

Luther clearly sees the didactic nature of history, but this he immediately follows with a theological twist in his conclusion:

> It all adds up to this: histories are nothing else than a demonstration, recollection, and sign of divine action and judgment, how [God] upholds, rules, obstructs, prospers, punishes, and honors the world, and especially men, each according to his just desert, evil or good (Luther, 1960, pp. 275-276).

In history we see man's actions and God's responses, both of grace (upholds, rules, prospers, honors) and of justice (obstructs, punishes.) History sets us in awe of our own decrepit sinfulness and God's unending mercy toward us.

In short, as with all good content in classical education, history pulls us outside ourselves. Its proper study chips away at the sinful nature's self-centeredness and places our lives in better perspective. Through history we see lowly men who have risen to power, and we see great men who have fallen. We see the decay of the sinful world, tempered by God's enduring grace toward mankind. With such a landscape on which to paint our own lives, we see how foolish it is to think too highly of ourselves, and yet we are also buoyed by the reassurance that God can and will use our lives, however humble or exalted they may appear, to His good and gracious purposes. This is the distinctly Lutheran view of history.

History is not on a level with infallible Scripture, though, and Luther cautions:

> . . . the greater number [of historians] write in such a way that they readily pass over or put the best construction on the vices and deficiencies of their own times in the interest of their lords or friends and in turn glorify all too highly some trifling or vain virtue. On the other hand, they embellish or besmirch histories to the advantage of their fatherland and disadvantage of the foreigners, according to whether they love or hate someone. In that way histories become extremely unreliable and God's work is shamefully obscured . . . Thus the noble, fine, and loftiest use of histories is ruined and they become nothing but bearers of gossip.

> . . . [However] we must remain satisfied with our historians as they are, and now and then reflect for ourselves and judge whether the writer is getting off the right track because of partiality or prejudice, whether he praises and blames too much or too little, according to

how he is disposed toward people or things, even as we must tolerate it that under a lax government teamsters along the way adulterate the wine with water, so that one cannot obtain a drink of pure vintage, and we must be satisfied with receiving the better part or something out of it (Luther, 1960, pp. 277-278).

The idea of bias coloring histories is nothing new. Luther recognized the impossibility of impartiality, but he believed that there is, in fact, truth underlying all our incomplete and imbalanced historical recordings and that its pursuit is a worthwhile endeavor. For the classical Lutheran teacher or student, the chain of history is not primarily one to bind us to our own time, nor primarily to link us with our past, though it does serve both these purposes. Instead, the chain of history is the craftsmanship of our God who has placed every link according to His goodness and justice, and from which, as the central ornament and meaning of all history, He hangs His cross in resplendent evidence of His grace toward mankind.

Finally, then, Luther speaks to the proper outlook on history:

. . . since histories describe nothing else than God's work, that is, grace and wrath, it is only right that one should believe them, as though they were in the Bible. They should therefore indeed be written [and we might add, taught] with the very greatest diligence, honesty, and truthfulness.

. . . in [history] one can indeed also see God's work, how marvelously he rules the children of men and how very wicked the devil is and all his, so that we learn to fear God and seek his counsel and aid in matters both large and small. To him be praise and thanks in all eternity, through our Lord Jesus Christ. Amen (Luther, 1960, pp. 277-278).

---

Heather Judd, B.A. in Education, M.A. in English, teaches at Mount Hope Lutheran School in Casper, Wyoming.

# IV. Classical Lutheran Education: Considerations for Today

Notes

## A Research Study: Effects of Classical Education on Achievement in Lutheran Schools

*by Anthony B. Splittgerber*

Classical education is (and remains!) a growing movement in education, but as a pedagogical model classical education has not often been researched quantitatively. Indeed, many of classical education's most compelling elements cannot be quantified. Although its core philosophies are highly compatible with Christian teachings, and many Christian schools have embraced classical education, classical education is not just for Christian schools. Classical education can be implemented by any school, and its proponents often tout both academic rigor and academic superiority. To the author's knowledge prior to this writing, there had never been published research to validate these assertions. There had, however, been several studies on the teaching of Latin (which all classical schools taught), with empirical evidence to suggest that students who study Latin fare far better on academic tests, especially in the language arts, than their counterparts who do not receive Latin instruction. Latin was but one component of the classical curriculum this research project studied.

The purpose of this study was to determine whether or not a significant difference existed in academic achievement between comparable Lutheran schools which utilized a classical education model and those that did not. This project analyzed standardized academic test scores to gauge the academic prowess of the classical education model within Lutheran schools.

A quasi-experimental design was selected for this project because assignment of groups would not be random, as would be the case in a true experiment. This project utilized a relatively small set of self-identified classical Lutheran schools. The researcher then sought to match each classical Lutheran school with a non-Lutheran counterpart. Random assignment was not an option if a sufficient amount of data was to be acquired.

This study utilized two subject test groups: a group of "classical Lutheran schools" and a counterpart group of "non-classical Lutheran schools." Initially, the first group would consist of 11 schools from the Consortium for Classical and Lutheran Education (CCLE). The schools were selected because of their curricular similarity and solidarity of beliefs and teaching, as evidenced by their membership in this consortium.

The selection of the second group, non-classical Lutheran schools, was made upon receipt of demographic data from the participating classical Lutheran schools. A concerted effort was made to find Lutheran schools that had similar total K-8 populations. Race, ethnicity, and gender were not factors of consideration in the selection of appropriate matches; instead, school population was the primary factor in determining matches, with geographic characteristics considered as well. For example, a classical Lutheran school with a student population of 60 students located in the Midwest would be matched with a non-classical counterpart with 60 students also located in the Midwest within a similar population setting, such as rural or urban.

Lutheran schools had been specifically chosen because of convenience – namely the accessibility, availability, and willingness of participants. With such a convenience sample it would become more difficult to assure that the sample was representative of the population; however, by using only Lutheran schools that were relatively geographically diverse (that is, schools not confined to a predetermined district or state), the degree of representation should have remained quite high because of the relative homogeneity of Lutheran schools.

This research project analyzed the results of standardized tests every school conducts annually. The data collection instrument for this project was the nationally-normed, standardized test administered for the 2008-2009 school year, such as either the Iowa Test of Basic Skills (ITBS) or some similar measure, such as the California Achievement Test (CAT). As long as the test used by each school was a nationally normed test, then the national percentile rankings (NPR's) of each test would remain comparable.

In order to compare the achievement of each school, this project focused on the national percentile rankings of each class per school in each subject. Paired classical and non-classical NPR's were compared. The NPR's of reading, language, math, and core tests in classical Lutheran schools were averaged, as were the NPR's of all non-classical schools. A t-test assessed the significance of the differences in NPR scores. Significance was determined at a .01 level due to the small sample size.

The comparison of means and the use of the t-test to evaluate significance answered the research question: *How do the standardized test scores of Lutheran classical schools compare to those of Lutheran schools not using the classical education model?* National percentile rankings were used because they were comparable to the percentile rankings in other similar tests. While stanines and grade equivalencies could also be compared, these scores were not as easily understood by the average reader as were national percentile rankings. In addition to the comparison of means, statistical analysis also included the mode, median, and range in an effort to elicit additional data for evaluation. These tools were examined for unexpected trends and to support the comparison of means and the use of the t-test.

The quasi-experimental design allowed for smaller sample populations, because various conditions limited the pool of available test subjects. In the end, six of the eleven classical schools participated with submission of their test scores. As it became clear that lower than expected numbers of classical Lutheran education schools would be participating, the research design was adjusted slightly to bolster the total number of participants in order to prevent invalidation of the research. To this end, each classical participant was matched with three to four potential matches in the hopes of strengthening the data with more participants. An emphasis would now be placed on the number of overall students in the pooled population of classical Lutheran schools and that of the non-classical Lutheran schools. Ultimately nine non-classical Lutheran schools agreed to participate in the study to be compared with six classical Lutheran schools.

An analysis of the data showed the following results. First, of the 36 subsets of data, only five of those subsets were statistically insignificant. Second, when one graphed the data by test type, one could see that at an early level, non-classical Lutheran schools outperformed classical Lutheran schools; however, the reverse happened for grades four through eight. From the fourth grade through the eighth grade, classical Lutheran schools outperformed non-classical schools in academic achievement as assessed through standardized testing. *In general, non-classical Lutheran schools' NPR's declined steadily from kindergarten through eighth grade while classical Lutheran schools' NPR's increased steadily from kindergarten through eighth grade.*

This researcher had hypothesized that the mean test scores of classical model schools would be significantly higher than non-classical schools. The research indicates that the hypothesis was an incorrect one – at least in part. The classical model schools did score higher than their non-classical counterparts in grades four through eight (with data statistically significant in all but the sixth grade). However, the hypothesis was incorrect in respect to the data for the lower grades, where the non-classical Lutheran schools performed significantly better than the classical schools.

Despite the partially incorrect hypothesis, the research was successful in answering the research question and in achieving the purpose of the research. There was most definitely a significant difference in achievement between the comparable Lutheran schools that utilized a classical education model and those that did not. The questions then became: *Why did the scores of the classical models begin so poorly in comparison to their later scores? Why did non-classical scores have such a decline from their kindergarten scores to their eighth grade scores?* These questions warrant further investigation.

It should be noted further that most classical schools did not begin the teaching of Latin until the third grade, which possibly explained why their scores continued a steady increase and overtook the non-classical schools in the fourth grade. In addition, most non-classical schools did not begin standardized testing until the third grade. From the third grade on, similar populations were being compared, but at the kindergarten level there were 94 classical students compared to only nine non-classical students. The non-classical score was extremely high (98th percentile) and was probably not representative of the entire non-classical population.

Classical Lutheran schools showed achievement gains in each of the four areas reported, even mathematics. This researcher had hypothesized that at the very least, classical Lutheran schools would show gains in reading and language, because previous research indicated that the teaching of Latin would have this effect. So it is some surprise that the classical school would still outperform the non-classical Lutheran school in the upper grades in mathematics. This data would give credence to the thought that it is the whole classical curriculum and pedagogy, not just the teaching of Latin, which helped to account for the difference in scores and the upward trend of the classical scores.

This research offers some preliminary quantitative data to demonstrate the effectiveness of classical education in areas of academic achievement. This research no doubt is not without error, and some may take issue with some assumptions this researcher has made. This researcher considers this research a starting point; perhaps others will expand on the research and further validate its results or refute them.

*Author's note: This article summarizes a much more thorough work. Research citations and references have been removed, as have all graphs, tables, and appendices. For those who wish to read the full, original research, a free download is available from this web address:

http://www.zionkearney.org/curriculum/academics/further-reading/

---

Mr. Anthony Splittgerber, B.S. Education and M.A. Elementary Administration from Concordia University Nebraska, serves as principal and teacher of Zion Lutheran School in Kearney, Nebraska.

Notes

## Best of Both Worlds: School/Home School Hybrid Model

*by Rev. Daniel Praeuner*

### Beginnings

Years ago when I served as senior pastor at Trinity Lutheran Church and School in Riverton, Wyoming, our school implemented classical and Lutheran education. When called by an older congregation in Roswell, New Mexico, I noted in the call documents a desire to start a school. It presented an opportunity to bring classical and Lutheran education to this community of 50,000 people.

Challenges faced us. Our older congregation had few young people. Of these, how many would be willing to transfer their children to a new school and pay tuition? In our community five private Christian schools already operated, and with average annual tuition of $3850 per student, some of these schools struggled. How could we do this? Should we even start, if we began with only a few children? How could we draw students from outside of the congregation? And what about staffing? Doubts multiplied. To add to our concern, our community's Christian churches leaned heavily Baptist, American Evangelical, or Roman Catholic. How would we overcome these challenges? Similar questions plague many Lutheran congregations.

### An Idea

I knew of a Christian school in Montana that operated successfully as a two-day private school and three-day home school. I also knew that classical Christian home schooling had proven effective for many families. If we combined private school and home school, could we have the best of both worlds?

Our feasibility committee began to discuss this model, and even the initially opposing members became enthusiastic. We designed a schedule, a curriculum, a budget, and a plan for physical classrooms. With sufficient financial support, we presented our model and specific proposals to the voter's assembly. We received approval. We appointed a Board of Education with its Chairman, our congregation's Education Chairman, as a Church Council position. The Board made plans for fall enrollment.

We had agreed that we would begin a school with as few as four students. Any less and we would wait another year. We began with our congregation's own young families. They voiced three concerns: expense, transitioning from current private and public schools to a new school, and a lack of parents' time to home school three days a week. When only one family agreed to enroll, the family's son would be our only student. We continued our search.

We advertised in the city newspaper and, with over two hundred homeschooling families in our community, we contacted the local homeschooling association. We invited the families to an informational meeting. When attendance exceeded our expectations, we prepared for an avalanche of enrollment; instead, many homeschoolers balked at surrendering their children two days a week. Only five children enrolled, all from two families, but we now had six students.

## A Teacher

It was time to call a teacher – a full-time teacher for six students!

*The teacher's schedule:*

- Monday/Wednesday 3 children (1 each in 1st, 2nd, 3rd grades)
- Tuesday/Thursday 3 children (1 each in 4th, 5th, 6th grades)
- Friday: teacher planning day

Finding a qualified teacher would prove to be the greatest obstacle so far. When I called Concordia Universities' placement offices to find a teacher for our classical school, I received no names. I phoned pastors and administrators who might know someone. Finally, someone provided us a name. A graduate of Concordia, Mequon, and a former student of Dr. Gene Edward Veith, she was familiar with classical education and had two years of teaching experience. We invited her for a visit and an interview. The voters extended a call, and she moved to New Mexico in the summer. We discussed curriculum options. Her first year she began with six students. With the financial gifts we had already secured, we paid her above District scale and gave her $300 each month as an endowment.

## Finances

As more enrolled, we reduced our operating costs. Today, six years later, we have 50 pre-K through 8th grade students enrolled for the 2012-2013 school year with costs of approximately $15,000. Over time our congregation has increased its investment in the school. Through an endowment, a gift will provide future income for the school. The Board of Education began an annual school fundraiser and offers a tuition assistance program for congregation members who cannot afford the school. Only one family has needed this assistance in the three years of its availability.

## Logistics

## Scheduling

- Pre-K children attend three mornings: Monday through Wednesday, 8 to noon.
- K-2 students attend two full days: Monday and Wednesday, 8:00 a.m. to 3:00 p.m. (These students attend on Friday whenever Monday is a holiday.)
- 3-5 and 6-8 students attend two full days: Tuesday and Thursday, 8:00 a.m. to 3:00 p.m.
- Most Fridays are teacher work days for planning, tutoring, or parent conferences.

## Work at Home

Teachers and parents work together. During the two days of school attendance, teachers instruct students in the curriculum, introduce concepts, engage in discussion, and evaluate for mastery of content. During the three days at home, parents teach and review with their children. Asked to arrange a separate school/study area in the home, parents are encouraged to spend at least four to five hours each of the three days at home with their student(s).

## Promotion

Most new students result from enthused families' referrals. We advertise in the newspaper late February our annual two-day March open house with school in session. As classes continue, teachers place sample curricula on tables in hallways. Volunteer parents register new students and answer questions. After this year's open house, eight new students enrolled. We offer an open house with classes in session! New homeschoolers and other interested parents visit while teachers conduct classes. The school's parents answer questions and display curricula on tables for the visitors.

## Testing

Every two years, we give Iowa standardized tests to help individual students and the school learn areas to improve.

## Family Interview

To ensure a family's success, we conduct a basic interview in which we ask the reason for enrolling the student and explain the dedication needed to home school three days each week. We impress upon them that we teach the Christian faith according to the Lutheran confessions. To date this has not deterred anyone. Where differences arise, families address these at home.

## Dress Code

Our students wear uniforms. We offer long- and short-sleeved polo shirts with our school logo. Both boys and girls wear khaki pants, or girls may wear khaki jumpers over their school shirts. No student may wear shorts or "flip-flop" shoes.

## Seven Tips for Starting A Classical Lutheran School/Home School

1. Understand that the main reason to start a school is to teach the faith. We instruct children how one's life in Christ permeates and drives everything you learn and do.

2. Be sure that at least 75% of your congregation wants to start a school. Some would suggest seeking 100% approval before beginning.

3. Have substantial seed money to begin your school. When schools start without adequate financial resources, by the end of the year a school can in such significant debt to require years to recover. This will greatly reduce congregational support. As you make plans for a school, build up a fund several years before you open.

4. Create a board wisely. Have parents whose children attend the school. Include a grandparent or two. Have your board chairman report directly to the church council and continuously apprise the congregation about the school. The board and teachers must be vigilant with congregational public relations, because most members do not have children in the school and attend only on Sundays.

5. Be sure the staff supports the school! As under-shepherd of the congregation, the pastor's involvement and enthusiasm will help others to be supportive. Try to find teachers trained in classical Lutheran education, and educate them so they can appreciate the benefits of a non-traditional school week. Consider training up teachers from within the congregation, perhaps with college scholarships to include teaching in the church's classical Lutheran school.

6. Begin with families who already home school. They will be interested. After a few enroll their students, more will follow.

7. Pray for God's direction and let Him take you where He leads. We started without a Pre-K, but in our second year, when school families and congregational families asked for this program, the Lord saw fit to bring to Roswell an LC-MS early childhood teacher eager to begin such a class. We have also had parents ask about high school. We trust in Him and continue to ask for His care and blessings.

## Summary

This model can fit perfectly with classical and Lutheran education. For congregations who would like to start a classical and Lutheran day school but are concerned about the cost, or for existing schools facing closing, this can be a viable alternative to the full-time school.

---

Longtime advocate of classical Lutheran education, the Reverend Daniel Praeuner is now in his eighth year with Immanuel Lutheran School in Roswell, New Mexico, where he lives with his wife Roxanne. Rev. Praeuner serves on the Board of the Consortium for Classical and Lutheran Education.

## A Book Review of Lutheran Education: From Wittenberg to the Future

*by Dr. Gene Edward Veith*

Thomas Korcok's history of Lutheran education shows that the classical liberal arts approach is not just another educational alternative with which some Lutherans, as well as other conservative Christians, are experimenting. With scholarship that will come as an eye-opening surprise even to advocates of classical education, Dr. Korcok shows that classical education combined with catechesis is *the* Lutheran educational tradition.

Moreover, he shows how this distinctively Lutheran approach to education is grounded in confessional Lutheran theology, to the point that throughout the history of Lutheranism—especially the strain that would become the Lutheran Church Missouri Synod—theological controversies were often played out not just in churches but in schools, curriculum, and pedagogy. Church leaders from Luther to Walther believed that the classical liberal arts integrated with catechesis was the educational model that could best equip church members to understand Lutheran theology and to serve their neighbors in their vocations.

Dr. Korcok, a pastor in the Lutheran Church of Canada, conducted this research for his doctoral dissertation at the Free University of Amsterdam. He begins with an illuminating account of how the fathers of the early church—especially St. Augustine—Christianized the Greco-Roman educational program designed for the free citizen (the *artes liberalis*), as opposed to the manual training given to tradesmen and slaves. This included the insight that the best of secular culture could be used by Christians in service to Christ. This tradition of Christian classicism was systematized further in the Middle Ages, with the invention of the university, whose curriculum was organized around the Seven Liberal Arts (the *trivium*, with its three language-related arts of grammar, logic, and rhetoric; and the *quadrivium*, with its four mathematics-related arts of arithmetic, geometry, music, and astronomy) and the three classifications of knowledge (*scientia*): Natural Science, Moral Science, and Theological Science.

Medieval scholasticism emphasized logic above the other liberal arts, but the Renaissance educational reforms emphasized the importance of rhetoric, which included the study of literature and the use of original sources—such as the Bible. It was in the context of Renaissance liberal arts education that the University of Wittenberg was founded and that the Reformation took place. A major priority for Luther and Melanchthon was the establishment of schools. These went beyond simply teaching Christians how to read the Bible. They also implemented a liberal arts curriculum, thus opening up an education designed to cultivate intellectual growth, creativity, and freedom to all Christians, including women, peasants, and others marginalized under feudal society.

The new Reformation schools were built upon two theological foundations. The first is Baptism. All Christians, by virtue of their Baptism, are priests in Christ's church. As Luther says in *The Babylonian Captivity of the Church*, in the church there is no "difference between laymen and priests, princes and bishops, between religious and secular, except for the sake of office and work, but not for the sake of status." This leveling effect meant, in the words of Dr. Korcok, that "if education in the liberal arts was suitable for the child of a prince, then it was suitable for the child of a laborer as well." The connection between Baptism and a liberal arts education was further developed by Johannes Bugenhagen, whose contribution to Lutheran education, Korcok shows, rivaled that of Melanchthon. The other key theological foundation to Lutheran education and the distinct shape that it assumed is the doctrine of vocation. Christians must be equipped to serve in both of God's Kingdoms. A liberal arts education, Luther and his fellow Reformers believed, best equips Christians for service to their neighbor in each of the estates to which God assigns us: not only the workplace (as in the current meaning of "vocational education"), but also in the family, the church, and the state.

Dr. Korcok shows that the theological conflicts faced by the Lutherans often manifested themselves in educational controversies. The Enthusiasts considered the liberal arts to be too worldly and wanted education that was restricted to learning how to read the Bible. On the other extreme, the Renaissance humanists believed that a liberal arts education is sufficient in itself to teach religion and good morals. No, said the Lutherans, the liberal arts by themselves, while valuable gifts of God, are not enough. Christians also need thorough catechesis in the revelations of Scripture and the truths of theology. The Pietists would also have an educational agenda. They, like the Enthusiasts, disapproved of the "pagan" and "worldly" scope of the classical liberal arts. They also had a more narrow understanding of vocation than the orthodox Lutherans, taking it only to mean "job" or "occupation." The Pietists wanted pragmatic schools that emphasized job training. Then came the Rationalists who wanted to throw out the liberal arts as relics of the past in favor of a new "scientific" education, which, ominously, would be combined with an emphasis on German nationalism. In each case, orthodox Lutherans defended and put into practice an education that combined the liberal arts with Lutheran catechesis.

Dr. Korcok makes an important contribution to the history of Lutheranism in America by showing that a major catalyst for the Saxon migration, in which confessional Lutherans fled the Prussian Union of the state church for America and other countries, was the condition of the schools. Confessional congregations generally managed to practice their Lutheran faith, despite the forced union with Reformed congregations, but they could not control the schools, which were dominated by Enlightenment rationalism, and they were appalled by the secularist education their children were receiving. The desire to give their children a truly Lutheran education—consisting of the liberal arts plus catechesis—was enough to make them leave their homeland in search of both religious and educational freedom.

Dr. Korcok documents how this distinctly Lutheran brand of education was a major priority for C. F. W. Walther and the other fathers of the Lutheran Church Missouri Synod. The book explores Walther's extensive writings on education and describes the early schools and educational projects of the newly-formed synod. These included the founding of *gymnasia*, the full-blown six-year classical high schools as devised by Melanchthon and that still to this day educate Germany's elite. These schools were primarily for church workers, young men who wished to prepare for the pastoral ministry with further seminary training and those who desired to become teachers. The ordinary parochial schools in virtually every parish were not on this level, doing far less with Latin and Greek and for a smaller period of time, but they were nevertheless academically impressive. In the 19th century, the fabled one-room schoolhouse was presided over by a teacher who herself barely had an elementary education; but the German immigrants who were going to Lutheran schools were taught by a thoroughly-trained, superbly-educated professional teacher, who worked from an academically rigorous curriculum. Dr. Korcok argues that the material success of the German immigrants in the 19th century, in contrast to those of other countries, owed a great deal to the quality of the education they were receiving in Lutheran schools.

Eventually, the distinctively classical quality of Lutheran schools started to fade. The pioneering Missouri Synod educators J. C. W. Lindemann and C. A. T. Selle, who founded in 1865 the teachers' seminary in Addison, Illinois (now Concordia University Chicago), did not themselves have a classical education. Though the gymnasia, such as the boarding schools in Milwaukee (now Concordia University Wisconsin) and St. Paul, Minnesota (now Concordia University St. Paul), continued to prepare future pastors with the classical languages, the typical parish school dropped Latin in favor of English. Dr. Korcok argues that just as Latin prepared students for participation in intellectual and cultural life of Medieval and Renaissance Europe, English played that same function for German immigrants. Dr. Korcok challenges the conventional view that Missouri Synod schools simply wanted to retain the German language as a way to preserve their German culture. Instead, these schools, while keeping the immigrants' native language alive—which was also the language of Lutheran theology—did a great deal to promote assimilation to American culture. German nationalism, again, was an unwelcome fixture of the rationalist education they were trying to escape. These German schools made a point of teaching English, which, again, contributed to the unusual success of this particular immigrant group. Still, the decline of Latin marked a decline in the classical quality of these schools, though in other ways the heritage of the liberal arts remained. Dr. Korcok does not deal with the more recent history of Lutheran education, with the eventual acceptance of John Dewey's "progressive" education program in the synod's teacher colleges and the impulse to follow the lead of American public schools in their approach to education, with catechesis remaining as the sole remaining Lutheran distinctive.

Today, as public education seems to have lost its way—to the point of exhibiting the anti-intellectualism of the Enthusiasts, the social engineering of the Humanists, the economic preoccupations of the Pietists, and the crass materialism of the Rationalists, all at the same time—many educators are rediscovering again the virtues of classical liberal arts education. Dr. Korcok's book is an important scholarly contribution to that effort. For Lutheran classical educators, it is the book they have been waiting for.

---

Dr. Gene Edward Veith is Provost and Professor of Literature at Patrick Henry College. Founding member and Board member of the Consortium for Classical and Lutheran Education, he is the author of many books including *Classical Education* and *God at Work: Your Christian Vocation in All of Life*.

Notes

V. Conclusions: For the Sake of Our Baptized Children

Notes

## Luther on Classical Lutheran Education

*by Rev. John Hill*

The following treatise is a chronologically arranged compilation of quotations from the writings of Dr. Martin Luther concerning schools, Christian education, and classical education. The comments of the present author are only intended to guide the reader from quotation to quotation with sufficient context for clarity of understanding. The reader is urged to read the texts for himself, if not in the original, then at least in the noted translation.

The evidence of Luther's own classical education is readily seen in his writings and documented in biographies and histories of the Reformation. Of particular interest for Luther's early examination of the integration of Scriptures and the seven liberal arts is his use of Cassiodorus' *Explanation of the Psalms*. Cassiodorus' commentary on the Psalms is an argument for the Christian use of the classical tradition, which Luther digested thoroughly at the beginning of his career as a lecturer in 1513-15, and the work is echoed in Luther's school treatises of the 1520s.

Luther's first formal treatment of the topic of schools is found in his treatise of 1520, "To the Christian Nobility". (Luther, 1995, vol. 44, pp. 123-217) This work is one of Luther's most important in the early reformation, and while tearing down the walls behind which papal authority was ensconced, he also proposed a lengthy list of reforms throughout the German states. The proposal on education (Luther, 1995, pp. 200-207) is directed primarily at the universities.

> The universities, too, need a good, thorough reformation. I must say that, no matter whom it annoys. Everything the papacy has instituted and ordered serves only to increase sin and error. What else are the universities, unless they are utterly changed from what they have been hitherto, than what the book of Maccabees calls *gymnasia epheborum et graecae gloriae* [i.e. places for the training of youth in the fashions of Greek culture. Cf. II Macc. 4:9]? What are they but places where loose living is practiced, where little is taught of the Holy Scriptures and the Christian faith, and where only the blind, heathen teacher Aristotle rules far more than Christ? In this regard my advice would be that Aristotle's *Physics, Metaphysics, Concerning the Soul, and Ethics*, which hitherto have been thought to be his best books, should be completely discarded along with all the rest of his books that boast about nature, although nothing can be learned from them either about nature or the Spirit. Moreover, nobody has yet understood him, and many souls have been burdened with fruitless labor and study, at the cost of much precious time. (Luther, 1995, vol. 44, p. 200)

Luther's objection to these works of Aristotle reveal that his reforms of the educational system at that time were not merely a blind return to ancient things, though he praised the ancient pedagogy in the liberal arts very highly, as will be seen below. His proposals for reform were guided primarily by theological criteria. He illustrated his objection to Aristotle, continuing with this very pointed rejection.

> For the same reasons his book on ethics is the worst of all books. It flatly opposes divine grace and all Christian virtues, and yet it is considered one of his best works. Away with such books! Keep them away from Christians. No one can accuse me of overstating the case,

or of condemning what I do not understand. Dear friend, I know what I am talking about. I know my Aristotle as well as you or the likes of you. I have lectured on him [Aristotle's *Nicomachean Ethics* four times a week during his first year, 1508-09] and been lectured on him, and I understand him better than St. Thomas or Duns Scotus did. I can boast about this without pride and if necessary, I can prove it. It makes no difference to me that so many great minds have devoted their labor to him for so many centuries. Such objections do not disturb me as once they did, for it is plain as day that other errors have remained for even more centuries in the world and in the universities.

I would gladly agree to keeping Aristotle's books, *Logic, Rhetoric, and Poetics,* or at least keeping and using them in an abridged form, as useful in training young people to speak and to preach properly. But the commentaries and notes must be abolished, and as Cicero's *Rhetoric* is read without commentaries and notes, so Aristotle's *Logic* should be read as it is without all these commentaries. (Luther, 1995, p. 201)

Luther continued with a recommendation of the languages and all of the seven liberal arts.

In addition to all this there are, of course, the Latin, Greek, and Hebrew languages, as well as the mathematical disciplines and history. But all this I commend to the experts. In fact, reform would come of itself if only we gave ourselves seriously to it. Actually a great deal depends on it, for it is here in the universities that the Christian youth and our nobility, with whom the future of Christendom lies, will be educated and trained. Therefore I believe that there is no work more worthy of pope or emperor than a thorough reform of the universities. And on the other hand, nothing could be more devilish or disastrous than unreformed universities. (Luther, 1995, p. 202)

Luther left the reform of the faculties in medicine to the medical men. He took a direct lead in the areas of law and theology, however, where he utterly rejected the study of canon law, especially the papal decrees. He urged that the theologians lecture primarily on Holy Scriptures, and beyond that, only the best books should be published and read. He stated,

The number of books on theology must be reduced and only the best ones published. It is not many books that make men learned, nor even reading. But it is a good book frequently read, no matter how small it is, that makes a man learned in the Scriptures and godly. Indeed, the writings of all the holy fathers should be read only for a time so that through them we may be led into the Scriptures. As it is, however, we only read them these days to avoid going any further and getting into the Bible. We are like men who read the sign posts and never travel the road they indicate. Our dear fathers wanted to lead us to the Scriptures by their writings, but we use their works to get away from the Scriptures. Nevertheless, the Scripture alone is our vineyard in which we must all labor and toil. (Luther, 1995, p. 205)

He then continued by urging that the Scriptures be the primary text in the schools at every level.

> Above all, the foremost reading for everybody, both in the universities and in the schools, should be Holy Scripture-and for the younger boys, the Gospels. And would to God that every town had a girls' school as well, where the girls would be taught the gospel for an hour every day either in German or in Latin. Schools indeed! Monasteries and nunneries began long ago with that end in view, and it was a praiseworthy and Christian purpose. . . . Is it not right that every Christian man know the entire holy gospel by the age of nine or ten? Does he not derive his name and his life from the gospel? (Luther, 1995, pp. 205-06)

He poured out a lament for the failures of the educational system of his day.

> Oh, we handle these poor young people who are committed to us for training and instruction in the wrong way! We shall have to render a solemn account of our neglect to set the word of God before them. Their lot is as described by Jeremiah in Lamentations 2 [:11-12], "My eyes are grown weary with weeping, my bowels are terrified, my heart is poured out upon the ground because of the destruction of the daughter of my people, for the youth and the children perish in all the streets of the entire city. They said to their mothers, 'Where is bread and wine?' as they fainted like wounded men in the streets of the city and gave up the ghost on their mothers' bosom." We do not see this pitiful evil, how today the young people of Christendom languish and perish miserably in our midst for want of the gospel, in which we ought to be giving them constant instruction and training. (Luther, 1995, p. 206)

Luther continued by putting forth his view on how enrollment standards should be managed at the universities.

> Moreover, even if the universities were diligent in Holy Scripture, we need not send everybody there as we do now, where their only concern is numbers and where everybody wants a doctor's degree. We should send only the most highly qualified students who have been well trained in the lower schools. (Luther, 1995, p. 206)

Finally, Luther concluded his recommendations for the reform of the universities with this oft-quoted and very important statement.

> I would advise no one to send his child where the Holy Scriptures are not supreme. Every institution that does not unceasingly pursue the study of God's word becomes corrupt . . . . I greatly fear that the universities, unless they teach the Holy Scriptures diligently and impress them on the young students, are wide gates to hell. (Luther, 1995, p. 207)

In 1523 Luther received a poem written by Eoban Koch (Eobanus Hessus, 1488-1540),a Latin professor at the University of Erfurt. The poem, called *Captiva* by Luther, praised Luther and the Reformation and indicated Hessus' support of the Reformation. In a letter of response dated March 29, 1523 (Luther, 1995, vol. 49, pp. 32-35), Luther presented his conviction that the recovery of "letters," the liberal arts identified with the humanism of his day, were a necessary prerequisite to the Reformation.

I myself am convinced that without the knowledge of the [Humanistic] studies [Latin *literae* for *bonae literae*], pure theology can by no means exist, as has been the case until now: when the [Humanistic] studies were miserably ruined and prostrate [theology] declined and lay neglected. I realize there has never been a great revelation of God's Word unless God has first prepared the way by the rise and the flourishing of languages and learning, as though these were forerunners, a sort of [John] the Baptist. Certainly I do not intend that young people should give up poetry and rhetoric. I certainly wish there would be a tremendous number of poets and orators, since I realize that through these studies, as through nothing else, people are wonderfully equipped for grasping the sacred truths, as well as for handling them skillfully and successfully. Of course, wisdom makes the tongues of infants eloquent; but [wisdom] does not wish the gift of language to be despised. Therefore I beg also you to urge your young people at my request (should this have any weight) to study poetry and rhetoric diligently.

Luther's initial 1520 proposal for education was preliminary at best and was merely one part of a larger tractate on the reform of the German states. As the Reformation progressed, the competing interests of the church, scholasticism, humanism, and the economic lure of trade were preventing the needs of community, church, and home from being met by a crumbling and ineffective educational system. In fact, Luther himself was being quoted as opposing the theologically corrupt schools, and his translation of Scriptures into the vernacular seemed to de-emphasize the importance of the languages. Genuine theological opposition to education was being urged by the radical reformers, who declared all learning sinful and devilish. This situation prompted Luther's 1524 treatise, "To the Councilmen of All Cities in Germany that they Establish and Maintain Christian Schools" .(Luther, 1995, vol. 45, p. 347-78) The advice that he gave in this work is practical in nature, leaving Melanchthon to systematize his suggestions, but they arose out of theology of the Lutheran Reformation and are presented as essential to it.

After a brief introduction which rooted the subsequent admonitions in the Gospel ("until Christ's righteousness goes forth as brightness, and His saving grace is lighted as a lamp,") (Luther, 1995, p. 347), Luther turned to the current condition of the schools.

First of all, we are today experiencing in all the German lands how schools are everywhere being left to go to wrack and ruin. The universities are growing weak, and monasteries are declining. . . . For now it is becoming known through God's word how un-Christian these institutions are, and how they are devoted only to men's bellies. . . No one is any longer willing to have his children get an education. "Why," they say, "should we bother to have them go to school if they are not to become priests, monks, or nuns? 'Twere better they should learn a livelihood to earn." (Luther, 1995, p. 348)

Luther observed that while the pre-Reformation educational system had served the devil by training people away from God's word and pure Gospel, the Reformation had revealed this deceit; now the complete rejection of education served the devil's evil purposes far better.

Luther then developed the theme of his treatise, the importance of the schools for the welfare of church and home and world. He does not speak of numbers, but of the one single student who can make all the difference.

> No one is on the alert, but just goes quietly along. Even though only a single boy could thereby be trained to become a real Christian, we ought properly to give a hundred gulden to this cause for every gulden we would give to fight the Turk, even if he were breathing down our necks. For one real Christian is better and can do more good than all the men on earth. (Luther, 1995, p. 350)

He urged the councilmen, as the keepers of the public purse, to make the funding of schools a great priority.

> For it is a grave and important matter, and one which is of vital concern both to Christ and the world at large, that we take steps to help our youth. . . . My dear sirs, if we have to spend such large sums every year on guns, roads, bridges, dams, and countless similar items to insure the temporal peace and prosperity of a city, why should not much more be devoted to the poor neglected youth—at least enough to engage one or two competent men to teach? (Luther, 1995, p. 350)

Luther further reminded them that the Christian has now been relieved of the vast financial burden of the Roman error. The money that had been spent for masses and pilgrimages should go to schools.

> Now that he is, by the grace of God, rid of such pillage and compulsory giving, he ought henceforth, out of gratitude to God and for his glory, to contribute a part of that amount toward schools for the training of the poor children. That would be an excellent investment. (Luther, 1995, p. 351)

Luther warned, however, that the German cities needed to seize the opportunity while they still had it.

> We have today the finest and most learned group of men, adorned with languages and all the arts, who could also render real service if only we would make use of them as instructors of the young people. Is it not evident that we are now able to prepare a boy in three years, so that at the age of fifteen or eighteen he will know more than all the universities and monasteries have known before? (Luther, 1995, p. 351)

He then reminded them that the freedom to provide sound Christian schooling was the very freedom of the Gospel itself, which they would not have forever. He sounded a reminder that rings prophetic for European and American Lutherans.

> For you should know that God's word and grace is like a passing shower of rain which does not return where it has once been. It has been with the Jews, but when it's gone it's gone,

and now they have nothing. Paul brought it to the Greeks; but again when it's gone it's gone, and now they have the Turk. Rome and the Latins also had it; but when it's gone, it's gone, and now they have the pope. And you Germans need not think that you will have it forever, for ingratitude and contempt will not make it stay. (Luther, 1995, pp. 352-53)

Luther then placed his greatest reason for the support of truly Christian schools before the councilmen.

The third consideration is by far the most important of all, namely the command of God, who through Moses urges and enjoins parents so often to instruct their children that Psalm 78 says: How earnestly he commanded our fathers to teach their children and to instruct their children's children [Ps. 78:5-6]. This is also evident in God's fourth commandment, in which the injunction that children shall obey their parents is so stern that he would even have rebellious children sentenced to death [Deut. 21:18-21]. Indeed, for what purpose do we older folks exist, other than to care for, instruct, and bring up the young? It is utterly impossible for these foolish young people to instruct and protect themselves. This is why God has entrusted them to us who are older and know from experience what is best for them. And God will hold us strictly accountable for them. (Luther, 1995, p. 353)

Luther listed three reason why parents neglect this duty and fail in their responsibility. He writes,

In the first place, there are some who lack the goodness and decency to do it, even if they had the ability. . . . In the second place, the great majority of parents unfortunately are wholly unfitted for this task. . . . In the third place, even if parents had the ability and desire to do it themselves, they have neither the time nor the opportunity for it, what with their duties and the care of the household. (Luther, 1995, p. 355)

Then he emphasized why this duty fell to the sound Christian councilmen of the cities of Germany to provide Christian schools, and why it was in their best interest to do so.

A city's best and greatest welfare, safety, and strength consist rather in its having many able, learned, wise, honorable, and well-educated citizens. They can then readily gather, protect, and properly use treasure and all manner of property.

So it was done in ancient Rome. There boys were so taught that by the time they reached their fifteenth, eighteenth, or twentieth year they were well versed in Latin, Greek, and all the liberal arts (as they are called), and then immediately entered upon a political or military career. Their system produced intelligent, wise, and competent men, so skilled in every art and rich in experience that if all the bishops, priests, and monks in the whole of Germany today were rolled into one, you would not have the equal of a single Roman soldier. As a result their country prospered; they had capable and trained men for every position. So at all times throughout the world simple necessity has forced men, even among the heathen, to maintain pedagogues and schoolmasters if their nation was to be brought to a high standard. Hence, the word "schoolmaster" is used by Paul in Galatians 4 as a word taken from the common usage and practice of mankind, where he says, "The law was our schoolmaster." (Luther, 1995, pp. 356)

With these lavish words of praise for the ancient, classical system of educating young men for the service of the nation, Luther then turned to the educational curriculum itself.

"All right," you say again, "suppose we do have to have schools; what is the use of teaching Latin, Greek, and Hebrew, and the other liberal arts? We could just as well use German for teaching the Bible and God's word, which is enough for our salvation." I reply: Alas! I am only too well aware that we Germans must always be and remain brutes and stupid beasts . . . . Languages and the arts, which can do us no harm, but are actually a greater ornament, profit, glory, and benefit, both for the understanding of Holy Scripture and the conduct of temporal government—these we despise. . . .

Truly, if there were no other benefit connected with the languages, this should be enough to delight and inspire us, namely, that they are so fine and noble a gift of God, with which he is now so richly visiting and blessing us Germans above all other lands. We do not see many instances where the devil has allowed them to flourish by means of the universities and monasteries; indeed, these have always raged against languages and are even now raging. For the devil smelled a rat, and perceived that if the languages were revived a hole would be knocked in his kingdom which he could not easily stop up again. Since he found he could not prevent their revival, he now aims to keep them on such slender rations that they will of themselves decline and pass away. (Luther, 1995, pp. 357-58)

Luther further reflected upon the importance of the humanist, Renaissance revival of the classical languages for the Reformation:

Although the gospel came and still comes to us through the Holy Spirit alone, we cannot deny that it came through the medium of languages, was spread abroad by that means, and must be preserved by the same means. For just when God wanted to spread the gospel throughout the world by means of the apostles he gave the tongues for that purpose. Even before that, by means of the Roman Empire he had spread Latin and Greek languages widely in every land in order that his gospel might the more speedily bear fruit far and wide. He has done the same thing now as well. Formerly no one knew why God had the languages revived, but now for the first time we see that it was done for the sake of the gospel, which he intended to bring to light and use in exposing and destroying the kingdom of Antichrist. . . . In proportion then as we value the gospel, let us zealously hold to the languages. (Luther, 1995, pp. 358-59)

Luther followed with praise for the Hebrew and Greek languages, because God chose them to be the languages in which His holy Word was given. He became eloquent in urging the teaching and learning of the sacred languages:

And let us be sure of this: we will not long preserve the gospel without the languages. The languages are the sheath in which this sword of the Spirit [Eph. 6:17] is contained; they are the casket in which this jewel is enshrined; they are the vessel in which this wine is held; they are the larder in which this food is stored; and, as the gospel itself points out [Matt. 14:20], they are the baskets in which are kept these loaves and fishes and fragments. (p. 360)

Luther had written something similar to the Bohemian Brethren at the end of his tract, "The Adoration of the Sacrament" (Luther, 1995, vol. 38, p. 304), urging them to train some of their talented boys in the Greek and Hebrew language.

Following a lengthy discussion of the importance of the languages especially for preachers of the Gospel, Luther then turned to the needs of the secular kingdom which must be supplied by good schools.

> To this point we have been speaking about the necessity and value of languages and Christian schools for the spiritual realm and the salvation of souls. Now let us consider also the body. Let us suppose that there were no soul, no heaven or hell, and that we were to consider solely the temporal government from the standpoint of its worldly functions. Does it not need good schools and educated persons even more than the spiritual realm? Hitherto, the sophists have shown no concern whatever for the temporal government, and have designed their schools so exclusively for the spiritual estate that it has become almost a disgrace for an educated man to marry. . . .(Luther, 1995, pp. 366-67)

Christian schools cannot be focused solely upon the spiritual realm, but must provide an education that serves the world. Here Luther again turned to the classical education of the ancient world.

> It is not necessary to repeat here that the temporal government is a divinely ordained estate . . . . The question is rather: How are we to get good and capable men into it? Here we are excelled and put to shame by the pagans of old, especially the Romans and Greeks. Although they had no idea of whether this estate were pleasing to God or not, they were so earnest and diligent in educating and training their young boys and girls to fit them for the task, that when I call it to mind I am forced to blush for us Christians, and especially for us Germans. Yet we know, or at least we ought to know, how essential and beneficial it is—and pleasing to God—that a prince, lord, councilman, or other person in a position of authority be educated and qualified to perform the functions of his office as a Christian should.

> Now if (as we have assumed) there were no souls, and there were no need at all of schools and languages for the sake of the Scriptures and of God, this one consideration alone would be sufficient to justify the establishment everywhere of the very best schools for both boys and girls, namely, that in order to maintain its temporal estate outwardly the world must have good and capable men and women, men able to rule well over land and people, women able to manage the household and train children and servants aright. Now such men must come from our boys, and such women from our girls. Therefore, it is a matter of properly educating and training our boys and girls to that end. (Luther, 1995, pp. 367-68)

This is the point where Luther then laid out his vision for a classical education in his day, rooted firmly in the pedagogical tradition that had been received through a thousand years of Christian adaptation from the Greeks and Romans.

> But if children were instructed and trained in schools, or wherever learned and well-trained schoolmasters and schoolmistresses were available to teach the languages [i.e. the trivium of

grammar, dialectic, and rhetoric], the other arts [i.e. the mathematical arts of the quadrivium], and history, they would then hear of the doings and sayings of the entire world, and how things went with various cities, kingdoms, princes, men, and women. Thus, they could in a short time set before themselves as in a mirror the character, life, counsels, and purposes—successful and unsuccessful—of the whole world from the beginning; on the basis of which they could then draw the proper inferences and in the fear of God take their own place in the stream of human events. In addition, they could gain from history the knowledge and understanding of what to seek and what to avoid in this outward life, and be able to advise and direct others accordingly. . . .

For my part, if I had children and could manage it, I would have them study not only languages and history, but also singing and music together with the whole of mathematics [i.e. the quadrivium: arithmetic, music, geometry, astronomy]. For what is all this but mere child's play? The ancient Greeks trained their children in these disciplines; yet they grew up to be people of wondrous ability, subsequently fit for everything. How I regret now that I did not read more poets [i.e. "literature"] and historians, and that no one taught me them! (Luther, 1995, pp. 368-70)

Luther understood the need for the children of that day to be home, do chores, and learn a trade, and consequently proposed that "study and work will go hand-in-hand while the boys are young and able to do both" (Luther, 1995, p. 370), and suggested likewise for the girls. He added, however,

The exceptional pupils, who give promise of becoming skilled teachers, preachers, or holders of other ecclesiastical positions, should be allowed to continue in school longer, or even be dedicated to a life of study. (Luther, 1995, p. 371)

Again he urged that action be taken quickly before it was too late.

The last section of this treatise took up the topic of books. Luther urged the collecting of libraries. Yet his prioritization also reveals the considerations that must go into the formation of a curriculum. He began with the importance of good books.

Finally, one thing more merits serious consideration by all those who earnestly desire to have such schools and languages established and maintained in Germany. It is this: no effort or expense should be spared to provide good libraries or book repositories, especially in the larger cities which can well afford it. For if the gospel and all the arts are to be preserved, they must be set down and held fast in books and writings. . . This is essential, not only that those who are to be our spiritual and temporal leaders may have books to read and study, but also that the good books may be preserved and not lost, together with the arts and languages which we now have by the grace of God. (Luther, 1995, p. 373)

Luther cited the example of Moses and the prophets. He also noted the failures of the monastic and university libraries, lamenting that "they taught us nothing good." He stated the indictment, "That is the reward of our ingratitude, that men failed to found libraries but let the good books perish and kept the poor ones."(Luther, 1995, p. 375)

Luther then gave a prioritized book list, a kind of curriculum, just as Cassiodorus had done 1000 years before him, as a suggested source for the program of education he envisioned.

> First of all, there would be the Holy Scriptures, in Latin, Greek, Hebrew, and German, and any other language in which they might be found. Next, the best commentaries, and, if I could find them, the most ancient, in Greek, Hebrew, and Latin. Then, books that would be helpful in learning the languages, such as the poets and orators, regardless of whether they were pagan or Christian, Greek or Latin, for it is from such books that one must learn grammar. After that would come books on the liberal arts, and all the other arts. Finally, there would be books of law and medicine; there too there should be careful choices among commentaries.

> Among the foremost would be the chronicles and histories, in whatever languages they are to be had. For they are a wonderful help in understanding and guiding the course of events, and especially for observing the marvelous works of God. How many fine tales and sayings we should have today of things that took place and were current in German lands, not one of which is known to us, simply because there was no one to write them down, and no one to preserve the books had they been written. (Luther, 1995, p. 376)

He concluded,

> Now that God has today so graciously bestowed upon us an abundance of arts, scholars, and books, it is time to reap and gather in the best as well as we can, and lay up treasure in order to preserve for the future something from these years of jubilee, and not lose this bountiful harvest. (Luther, 1995, p. 377)

One of the very significant events of the reformation was the first official visitation of the churches and schools of Electoral Saxony. The actual visitation began early in 1527. In the year that followed, Philip Melanchthon began to draw up a guide as the doctrinal foundation for the visitation. *Instructions for the Visitors of Parish Pastors in Electoral Saxony* (Luther, 1995, vol. 40, pp. 269-324) was prepared under Luther's observations and guidance, expressed his theology and ideas, and bore his preface. He personally revised later editions of the work. Finally, Instructions was fully endorsed by Luther. For these reasons the text is generally included in the works of Luther. It is included here to give the reader a fuller picture of the Lutheran reform of the classical, liberal arts education of the parish schools.

The final section of instructions for the visitor pertains to schools (Luther, 1995, pp. 314-24) and is quoted here at length. The opening words express the direct ideas of Luther as noted from other works of his concerning schools.

> The preachers are to exhort the people to send their children to school so that persons are educated for competent service both in church and state. For some suppose it is sufficient if

the preacher can read German, but this is a dangerous delusion. For whoever would teach another must have long practice and special ability which are achieved only after long study from youth on. As St. Paul says in 1 Tim. 3:2 A bishop must be capable to instruct and teach others. Thereby he shows that preachers must be better qualified than laymen. He praises Timothy in 1 Tim. 4:6 because he has been instructed from his youth, nourished on the words of the faith and of good doctrine. For it is not an insignificant art to teach others clearly and correctly, and it is not within the power of such folk as have no learning.

Able people of this kind are needed not only in the churches but God also desires them in secular government.

Because it is God's will, then, parents should send their children to school, and prepare them for the Lord God so that he may use them for the service of others. (Luther, 1995, p. 314)

Here the *Instructions* remind the visitors and parish pastors that the children are not sent to school for the sake of earning an income, but to prepare them for service. God "will provide for them as he has promised" (Luther, 1995, p. 315), they are reminded. The instructions then turn to the curriculum.

At present many faults exist in the schools. We have set up the following syllabus of study so that the youth may be rightly instructed.

In the first place the schoolmasters are to be concerned about teaching the children Latin only, not German or Greek or Hebrew as some have done hitherto and troubled the poor children with so many languages. This is not only useless but even injurious. . . .

Secondly, they are also not to burden the children with a great many books, but avoid multiplicity in every way possible.

Thirdly, it is necessary to divide the children into groups. (Luther, 1995, p. 315)

What follows are the three divisions recommended for the parish schools and the curriculum which was to be used.

The First Division

The first division consists of children who are beginning to read. Here this order should be followed.

They shall first learn to read the primer in which are found the alphabet, the Lord's Prayer, the Creed, and other prayers.

When they have learned this they shall be given Donatus [350 B.C., Roman grammarian and teacher of rhetoric; his Ars grammatica was a popular textbook of medieval schools] and Cato [100 B.C., Roman poet and teacher of grammar; grammar was largely the study of parts of speech, and was intended to enable the student to read Latin], to read Donatus and to expound Cato. The schoolmaster is to expound one or two verses at a time, and the children are to repeat these at a later time, so that they thereby build up a vocabulary of Latin words and get a supply of words for speaking.

They shall practice this until they can read well. We would consider it not unfruitful if the weaker children who do not have especially quick minds, went through Cato and Donatus not only once but also a second time.

The children are to be taught to write and be obliged to show their lessons daily to the schoolmaster.

In order that they may learn a greater number of Latin words, the children may be assigned a few words for memorization each evening, as wise teachers formerly have done in the schools.

These children shall also be taught music and shall sing with the others, as we hope by God's help to show later. (Luther, 1995, p. 315-16)

The *Instructions* then turn to the second stage of the parish schools and the formal beginning of the grammar stage of education.

The Second Division

The second division consists of those children who can read and should now learn grammar. With these we should proceed in the following manner.

All the children, large and small, should practice music daily, the first hour in the afternoon.

Then the schoolmaster shall first expound the fables of Aesop [about 600 B.C.; these stories have a moral and were often used in the Middle Ages as texts in the school] to the second division.

After vespers the *Paedagogia* of Mosselanus [1493-1524, humanist scholar and professor at Leipzig; his grammar, *Paedagogia*] should be explained and, these books learned, selections should be made from the *Colloquies* of Erasmus [1466-1563; a leader of the Renaissance revival; *Colloquies* were a collection of dialogues in which he caricatured superstitious practices], such as are useful and edifying for children.

This may be repeated on the following evening.

When the children go home in the evening a sentence from a poet or other writer may be prescribed which is to be repeated the next morning, such as *Amicus certus in re incerta cernitur:* A friend in need is a friend in deed. Or, *Fortuna quem nimium fovet, stultum facit:* Of him on whom fortune smiles too much it makes a fool. Also Ovid [43 B.C.-A.D.17], last of the great Roman poets; *Ars amatoria and Metamorphoses]: Vulgus amicitias utilitate probat:* The crowd praises friendship for its usefulness.

In the morning the children shall again explain Aesop.

The preceptor shall decline a number of nouns and [conjugate] verbs, many or few, easy or hard, according to the ability of the pupils, and have them give the rule or explanation of these forms.

When children have learned the rules of syntax they should be required in this period to identify parts of speech or to construe, as it is called, which is a very useful practice, though it is used by few.

When now the children have learned Aesop in this way, they are to be given Terence [ca. 190-ca. 159 B.C., Roman comic poet] to be learned by heart. For they have now matured and can carry more work. But the schoolmaster shall exercise care so that the children are not overtaxed.

After Terrence the children shall be given some of the fables of Plautus [d. 184 B.C., Roman comic dramatist who adapted Greek plays to the Roman stage], such as are not objectionable: *Aulularia, Trinummus, Pseudolus,* and the like.

The hours before noon shall always and everywhere be so ordered that only grammar be taught. First, etymology. Then, syntax. Next, prosody. When this is finished, the teacher should start over again from the beginning, giving the children a good training in grammar. For if this is not done all learning is lost labor and fruitless.

The children are to recite these grammatical rules from memory, so that they are compelled and driven to learn grammar well.

Where the schoolmaster shuns this kind of work, as is often the case, he should be dismissed and another teacher found for the children, who will take on this work of holding the children to grammar. For no greater harm can be done to all the arts than where the children are not well trained in grammar.

This is to be done all through the week, and the children are not to be assigned a new book every day.

But one day, for instance Saturday or Wednesday, shall be appointed on which the children are given Christian instruction.

For some are taught nothing out of holy Scripture. Some teach their children nothing but holy Scripture. We should yield to neither of these practices.

It is essential that the children learn the beginning of a Christian and blessed life. But there are many reasons why also other books beside Scripture should be given the children from which they may learn to speak.

This order should be followed: The schoolmaster shall have the whole division come up for recitation, asking each pupil in turn to repeat the Lord's Prayer, the Creed, and the Ten Commandments.

If the group is too large one part may come up for recitation one week, another the following.

In one period the schoolmaster should explain simply and correctly the meaning of the Lord's Prayer, at another time, the Creed, at another, the Ten Commandments. He should emphasize what is necessary for living a good life, namely, the fear of God, faith, good works. He should not touch on points of dissension. He also should not accustom the children to lampoon monks or others, as many incompetent teachers do.

Furthermore the teachers should ask the pupils to memorize a number of easy Psalms that contain in themselves a summary of the Christian life and speak about the fear of God, faith, and good works. (Luther, 1995, pp. 317-18)

Here the *Instructions* give psalms 112, 34, 128, 125, 127, and 133 as examples. It continues:

On these days, too, St. Matthew is to be expounded grammatically. When one has completed it, one should begin again from the beginning.

Or, if the boys are a little older, one may expound the two epistles of Paul to Timothy, or the first epistle of John, or the Book of Proverbs.

The schoolmaster should not undertake to read other books than these. For it is fruitless to burden the youth with hard and deep books. It is for their own reputation that some have assayed to read Isaiah, the Epistle of Paul to the Romans, the Gospel of St. John, and the like.

The Third Division

When now the children have been well drilled in grammar the more excellent ones may be chosen for a third group.

Along with the others these shall rehearse music the hour after noon.

Then one should expound Virgil [70–19 B.C., best known of the Roman poets; Eclogues, Georgics, and the Aeneid] to them, and when this is finished one may read Ovid's Metamorphoses with them.

In the evening: Cicero's *Officia* or *Familiar Letters* [106–43 B.C., Roman orator, politician, and philosopher].

In the morning: Virgil is to be repeated, and in grammar the pupils are to be required to explain, decline, and indicate the various forms of discourse.

One should keep to grammar the hours before noon, so that the pupils may be well drilled in this.

When they have mastered etymology and syntax the pupils shall go on to prosody, wherein they become accustomed to composing verses. For this practice is very useful in learning to understand other writings. Also it gives the pupils a rich vocabulary and makes them apt in many ways.

When they have sufficiently studied grammar they may use these hours for dialectic and rhetoric.

Of the second and third divisions should be required each week a written exercise such as a letter or a poem.

The pupils shall also be required to speak Latin. The schoolmaster himself, as far as possible, should speak only Latin with the pupils so that they become accustomed to and are encouraged in this practice. (Luther, 1995, pp. 319-20)

Appearing at about the same time as the Visitation Articles was Luther's 1528 *Confession Concerning Christ's Supper*. (Luther, 1995, vol. 37, pp. 161-372) In the first two parts of his Great Confession Luther responded to the fanatics on the doctrine of the Lord's Supper and examined in detail the four biblical texts of the Lord's Supper. In the third and final section, however, Luther set out to confess all the articles of the faith in a final and comprehensive way. This section became one of the foundation documents for the Schwabach articles of 1529, and in turn, of the Augsburg Confession.

In affirming the three "holy orders and true institutions established by God" (Luther, 1995, p. 364), namely, the office of priest or ministry of the Word, the estate of marriage, and the civil government, Luther rejected and condemned the monastic orders. However, he observed a continuing good use for these foundations, thus defining the central purposes of the schools.

It would be a good thing if monasteries and religious foundations were kept for the purpose of teaching young people God's Word, the Scriptures, and Christian morals, so that we might train and prepare fine, capable men to become bishops, pastors, and other servants of the church, as well as competent, learned people for civil government, and fine, respectable, learned women capable of keeping house and rearing children in a Christian way. But as a way of seeking salvation, these institutions are all the devil's doctrine and creed, 1 Timothy 4 [:1], etc. (Luther, 1995, p. 364)

The matter of the monasteries surfaced again in a letter from Margrave George of Brandenburg to Luther, reporting the reform of the churches throughout Brandenburg and asking his advice on the best way to correct the continuing abuses in the monasteries. Luther replied in a letter dated July 18, 1529. (Luther, 1955, pp. 325-27)

In the first place, we think it well that the monasteries and foundations should be left as they are until they die out, for so long as the old inmates still live, and they are forced either to introduce or put up with innovations, there is little hope that there will be any peace. Moreover, such worship, established on the foundation of the old manner of worship, will in time become an unprofitable thing, as has occurred before. Whatever of the old, good order of worship it is desired to reintroduce is best put into the schools and parish churches, where the common man too can be present and be touched by it, etc. as we do here in Wittenberg and in other towns.

In the second place, it would be good if in Your Grace's principality Your Grace would establish one or two universities, where not only the Holy Scriptures but also law and all the sciences would be taught. From these schools learned men could be got as preachers, pastors, secretaries, councilors, etc. for the whole principality. To this purpose the income of the monasteries and foundations could be applied so that good scholars could be maintained in the schools at proper salaries: two theologians, two jurists, one professor of medicine, one mathematician, and four or five men for grammar, logic, rhetoric, etc. If studying is to be encouraged, you must have, not empty cloisters and deserted monasteries and endowed churches, but a city in which many people come together, work together, and incite and stimulate one another. Solitary studies do not accomplish this, but common studies do, for where many are together one gives another incentive and example.

In the third place, it is well that in all towns and villages good primary schools be established. From these could be picked and chosen those who are fit for the universities, and men can then be taken from the universities who are to serve your land and people. If the towns or their citizens cannot do this, it would be well to establish new stipends for the support of a few bright fellows in the deserted monasteries, and so every town might have one or two students. In the course of time, when the common people see that their sons can become pastors and preachers and incumbents of other offices, many of those who now think that a scholar cannot get a living will again keep their sons in school.

If some of the scholars who are trained in these schools take service and hold office in the dominions of other princes, and the objection is made that you are training people for other lords, it must be remembered that this does no harm, for beyond a doubt these men will promote the founding and endowment of schools in the lands of other princes and peoples, etc. (Luther, 1955, pp. 326-27)

In a letter to Elector John of Saxony, written the next year (May 20, 1530), Luther gave strong encouragement to his lord to hold fast to the true confession and doctrine at the Diet of Augsburg. (Luther, 1955, pp. 140-144) He pointed to Christian schools and well-indoctrinated and pious children as the first and brightest evidence of the blessing of the pure Gospel being given full protection and support. He wrote,

> The merciful God is also giving a sign of his graciousness by making his Word so powerful and fruitful in Your Grace's land. For surely Your Grace's land has more excellent pastors and preachers than any other land in the whole world, and their faithful, pure teaching helps to preserve peace. As a consequence the tender youth, both boys and girls, are so well instructed in the Catechism and the Scriptures that I am deeply moved when I see that young boys and girls can pray, believe, and speak more of God and Christ than they ever could in the monasteries, foundations, and schools of bygone days, or even of our day.

> Truly Your Grace's land is a beautiful paradise for such young people. There is no other place like it in all the world. God has erected this paradise in Your Grace's land as a special token of his grace and favor. (Luther, 1955, pp. 142-43)

Luther again addressed the issue of education in the two catechisms of the Lutheran Church. In the preface to The Small Catechism (Preface 19-20, The Book of Concord: The Confessions of the Evangelical Lutheran Church, Robert Kolb and Timothy J. Wengert, eds., Fortress Press: Minneapolis, 2000), Luther wrote,

> In particular, at this point also urge governing authorities and parents to rule well and to send their children to school. Point out how they are obliged to do so and what a damnable sin they commit if they do not, for thereby, as the worst enemies of God and humanity, they overthrow and lay waste both the kingdom of God and the kingdom of the world. Explain very clearly what kind of horrible damage they do when they do not help to train children as pastors, preachers, civil servants, etc., and tell them that God will punish them dreadfully for this. For in our day and age it is necessary to preach about these things. The extent to which parents and governing authorities are now sinning in these matters defies description. The devil, too, intends to do something horrible in all this. (Kolb and Wengert, 2000, p. 350)

His instruction related to education is found in the Fourth Commandment of The Large Catechism (141 and 167-78, Ibid., pp. 405-10). Schools are included in the command and promise of the Fourth Commandment, in that teachers exercise a delegated authority. So Luther observed,

Where a father is unable by himself to bring up his child, he calls upon a schoolmaster to teach him; if he dies, he confers and delegates his responsibility and authority to others appointed for the purpose. (Luther, 1988, p. 141)

Luther turned to the duties of parents included under the Fourth Commandment. Here he laid out the vision of what must be done with children, how the parents should understand and approach their duty, and what the parents should hope to accomplish in their homes. Luther's teaching lays the foundation for the parents' attitude and use of the schools.

In addition, it would also be well to preach to parents on the nature of their responsibility, how they should treat those whom they have been appointed to rule. Although their responsibility is not explicitly presented in the Ten Commandments, it is certainly treated in detail in many other passages of Scripture. God even intends it to be included precisely in this commandment in which he speaks of father and mother. For he does not want scoundrels or tyrants in this office or authority; nor does he assign them this honor (that is, power and right to govern) so that they may receive homage. Instead, they should keep in mind that they owe obedience to God, and that, above all, they should earnestly and faithfully discharge the duties of their office, not only to provide for the material support of their children, servants, subjects, etc., but especially to bring them to the praise and honor of God. Therefore do not imagine that the parental office is a matter of your pleasure and whim. It is a strict commandment and injunction of God, who holds you accountable for it.

But once again, the real trouble is that no one perceives or pays attention to this. Everyone acts as if God gave us children for our pleasure and amusement, gave us servants merely to put them to work like cows or donkeys, and gave us subjects to treat as we please, as if it were no concern of ours what they learn or how they live. No one is willing to see that this is the command of the divine Majesty, who will solemnly call us to account and punish us for its neglect. Nor is it recognized how very necessary it is to devote serious attention to the young. For if we want capable and qualified people for both the civil and the spiritual realms, we really must spare no effort, time, and expense in teaching and educating our children to serve God and the world. We must not think only of amassing money and property for them. God can provide for them and make them rich without our help, as indeed he does daily. But he has given us children and entrusted them to us precisely so that we may raise and govern them according to his will; otherwise, God would have no need of fathers and mothers. Therefore let all people know that it is their chief duty—at the risk of losing divine grace—first to bring up their children in the fear and knowledge of God, and, then, if they are so gifted, also to have them engage in formal study and learn so that they may be of service wherever they are needed.

If this were done, God would also bless us richly and give us grace so that the people might be trained who would be a credit to the nation and its people. We would also have good, capable citizens, virtuous women who, as good managers of the household [Titus 2:5], would faithfully raise upright children and servants. Think what deadly harm you do when you are negligent and fail to bring up your children to be useful and godly. You bring upon yourself sin and wrath, thus earning hell by the way you have reared your own children, no matter how holy and upright you may be otherwise. Because this commandment is neglected, God also terribly punishes the world; hence there is no longer any discipline, government, or peace. We all complain about this situation, but we fail to see that it is our own fault. We have unruly and disobedient subjects because of how we train them. This is enough to serve as a warning; a more extensive explanation will have to await another time. (Luther, 1988, pp. 167-78, pp. 409-10)

The "another time" came in the next year, 1530. Six years after "To the Noblemen", while the Diet at Augsburg was in session, Luther used his enforced idleness at the Coburg to address the problem of parents taking their students out of school in favor of "trade and commerce". The tract, entitled "A Sermon on Keeping Children in School", (Luther, 1995, vol. 46, pp. 213-58) includes a fine description and encomium of the pastoral office and its great importance for both church and state. Luther especially condemned the materialism that led parents to focus only on the economic success of their children instead of providing for the needs of church and state. In praising the city of Nurnberg in the opening pages, Luther noted,

There may, of course, be an occasional idolater, a servant of Mammon [Matt. 6:24], who will take his son out of school and say, "If my son can read and do arithmetic, that is enough; we now have books in German, etc." Such a person sets a bad example for all the other good citizens. (Luther, 1995, p. 215)

Luther then urged the pastors and preachers especially to take a leadership role in exhorting parents to keep their children in school, lest the devil "have his own way with our offspring," and "the Scriptures and learning disappear".(Luther, 1995, p. 217) He indicated the shape of this education in condemning their reluctance to pay for the right teachers.

Because they are not now willing to support and keep the honest, upright, virtuous school-masters and teachers offered them by God to raise their children in the fear of God, and in virtue, knowledge, learning, and honor by dint of hard work, diligence and industry, and at small cost and expense, they will get in their place incompetent substitutes, ignorant louts such as they have had before, who at great cost and expense will teach the children nothing but how to be utter asses. (Luther, 1995, p. 218)

Luther's declaration of the law was unyielding as he condemned the educational priority of getting the child a good, well-paying job:

He has not given you your children and the means to support them simply so that you may do with them as you please, or train them just to get ahead in the world. You have been earnestly commanded to raise them for God's service, or be completely rooted out—you, your children, and everything else, in which case everything you have done for them is condemned. (Luther, 1995, p. 222)

The first portion of Luther's exhortation placed the highest priority on providing pastors for the church, along with sacristans and schoolmasters. Church offices need well-educated men.

> Boys of such ability ought to be kept at their studies, especially sons of the poor, for all the endowments and revenues of the foundations and monasteries are earmarked for this purpose. In addition, though, other boys as well ought to study, even those of lesser ability. They ought at least to read, write, and understand Latin, for we need not only highly learned doctors and masters of Holy Scripture but also ordinary pastors who will teach the gospel and the catechism to the young and ignorant, and baptize and administer the sacrament. . . .

> Even though a boy who has studied Latin should afterward learn a trade and become a craftsman, he still stands as a ready reserve in case he should be needed as a pastor or in some other service of the word. Neither will such knowledge hurt his capacity to earn a living. On the contrary, he can rule his house the better because of it . . . . (Luther, 1995, p. 231)

Following a lengthy section on the spiritual office of preaching, Luther turned to providing for temporal or worldly government, which is also an ordinance and gift of God. (Luther, 1995, p. 237) He defined this government and observed that it is ruled most effectively by wisdom, not by force. (Luther, 1995, p. 238) As he had praised the good done by the preaching office, so he also praised the good that the pious jurist, legal scholar, or clerk can do. (Luther, 1995, p. 240) "All these great works your son can do. He can become such a useful person if you will hold him to it and see him educated". (Luther, 1995, p. 241) He compared the two offices:

> Indeed, there is need in this office for abler people than are needed in the office of preaching, so it is necessary to get the best boys for this work; for in the preaching office Christ does the whole thing, by his Spirit, but in the worldly kingdom men must act on the basis of reason—wherein the laws also have their origin—for God has subjected temporal rule and all of physical life to reason (Genesis 2 [:15]). (Luther, 1995, p. 242)

Here Luther also inserted a brief comment on the singular pleasure that education provides:

> I shall say nothing here about the pure pleasure a man gets from having studied, even though he never holds an office of any kind, how at home by himself he can read all kinds of things, talk and associate with educated people, and travel and do business in foreign lands; for there are perhaps very few people who are moved by this pleasure. (Luther, 1995, p. 243)

In this section of his sermon Luther especially praised the laws of the land and those whose work is the making and upholding of lawful rule. He also praised the work of soldiers, and then made a statement that reinforced the important point that education should not make the distinctions of elite and despised classes of people or vocations, but should enable men to recognize the value of each vocation.

Every occupation has its own honor before God, as well as its own requirements and duties. . . . All the estates and works of God are to be praised as highly as they can be, and not despised in favor of another. For it is written, *"Confessio et magnificentia opus ejus,"* "What God does is fine and beautiful", and again in Psalm 104[:31], "God rejoices in his works." These ideas ought to be impressed particularly by the preachers on the people from their youth up, by schoolmasters on their boys, and by parents on their children, so that they may learn well what estates and offices are God's, ordained by God, so that once they know this they will not despise or ridicule or speak evil of any one of them but hold them all in high regard. That will both please God and serve the cause of peace and unity, for God is a great lord and has many kinds of servants.(Luther, 1995, p. 246)

Luther observed further that these estates and offices will have wicked people in them, but that the offices themselves continue to be God's institution, and should not be despised just because wicked people do not use them with honor. Furthermore he warned against comparing the difficulty of one vocation against another. In this context he reflected on his own office as a writer, a vocation directly taught and developed in school.

But in writing, the best part of the body (which is the head) and the noblest of the members (which is the tongue) and the highest faculty (which is speech) must lay hold and work as never before. . . . They say of writing that "it only takes three fingers to do it"; but the whole body and soul work at it too. (Luther, 1995, p. 249)

He even indulged in personal reflections on how his education at Eisenach and Erfurt brought him to where he was. He noted,

I have come so far by means of the writer's pen—as this psalm [113:5-8] says—that I would not now change places with the Turkish sultan, giving up my knowledge for all his wealth. Indeed, I would not exchange what I know for all the wealth in the world multiplied many times over. Without any doubt, I should not have come to this if I had not gone to school and become a writer. (Luther, 1995, p. 251)

To this point Luther focused generally upon vocations related to preaching and government. He then pointed out also the other fields that require education.

At this point I should also mention how many educated men are needed in the fields of medicine and the other liberal arts. Of these two needs one could write a huge book and preach for half a year. Where are the preachers, jurists, and physicians to come from, if grammar and other rhetorical arts are not taught? For such teaching is the spring from which they all must flow. To speak of this here in detail would be too big a task. I will simply say briefly that a diligent and upright schoolmaster or teacher, or anyone who faithfully trains and teaches boys, can never be adequately rewarded or repaid with any amount of money, as even the heathen Aristotle says. . . . I know that next to that of preaching, this is the best, greatest, and most useful office there is. (Luther, 1995, pp. 252-53)

Luther's closing words brought the heart of the sermon to its conclusion. In the context of close inter-dependence of church and state, Luther gave this pronouncement:

> But I hold that it is the duty of the temporal authority to compel its subjects to keep their children in school, especially the promising ones we mentioned above. For it is truly the duty of government to maintain the offices and estates that have been mentioned, so that there will always be preachers, jurists, pastors, writers, physicians, schoolmasters, and the like, for we cannot do without them. (Luther, 1995, p. 256)

Again, he emphasized the gravity of the need for sound education:

> For here there is a worse war on, a war with the very devil, who is out to secretly sap the strength of the cities and principalities, emptying them of their able persons until he has bored out the pith and left only an empty shell of useless people whom he can manipulate and toy with as he will. That is, indeed, to starve out a city or a land and destroy it without a battle, before anyone is even aware of what is going on. (Luther, 1995, p. 257)

Finally, he urged that just as the able boys are to be sent to school, so the wealth of both the church and the church members should be used to bring about this education.

> Therefore let everyone be on his guard who can. Let the government see to it that when it discovers a promising boy he is kept in school. If the father is poor, the resources of the church should be used to assist. Let the rich make their wills with this work in view, as some have done who have established scholarship funds. This is the right way to bequeath your money to the church, for this way you do not release departed souls from purgatory but, by maintaining God's offices, you do help the living and those to come who are yet unborn, so that they do not get into purgatory, indeed, so that they are redeemed from hell and go to heaven; and you help the living to enjoy peace and happiness. That would be a praiseworthy Christian testament. God would have delight and pleasure in it, and would bless and honor you in return by giving you pleasure and joy in him. (Luther, 1995, p. 257)

Another brief snapshot of Luther's continuing advocacy in the transition from monastery schools to genuinely Lutheran schools (1537) may be seen in the Smalcald Articles (II.iii.1, Kolb, p. 306).

> That foundations and monasteries, established in former times with good intentions for the education of learned people and decent women, should be returned to such use so that we may have pastors, preachers, and other servants of the church, as well as other people necessary for earthly government in cities and states, and also well-trained young women to head households and manage them.

In the final years of his life (1539) Luther wrote "On the Councils and the Church", (Luther, 1995, vol 41, pp. 9-178) one of his most important writings, a work that deserves more reading and study than it often receives. In it, Luther resisted the overblown claims of church councils, and observed how councils must relate to the local congregation and its school. He wrote:

Do you think then that the offices of the pastor and the schoolteacher are so low that they cannot be compared with the councils? How could one assemble a council if there were no pastors or bishops? How could we get pastors if there were no schools? I am speaking of those schoolteachers who instruct the children and the youth not only in the arts, but also train them in Christian doctrine and faithfully impress it upon them; I also speak in the same manner of pastors who teach God's word in faithfulness and purity. (Luther, 1995, p. 132)

Luther went on to compare church councils with the supreme court of an empire, with the ancient law of this empire being the Holy Scriptures. He noted, "Not only the council, but every pastor and schoolteacher is also the servant or judge of this law and empire". (Luther, 1995, p. 133) He observed that in the empire of the world the laws change with the changing times. But not so in the church:

But in this empire of the church the rule is, "The word of our God will stand for ever" [Isa. 40:8]. One has to live according to it and refrain from creating new or different words of God and from establishing new and different articles of faith. That is why pastors and schoolteachers are the lowly, but daily, permanent, eternal judges who anathematize without interruption, that is, fend off the devil and his raging. A council, being a great judge, must make old, great rascals pious or kill them, but it cannot produce any others. A pastor and a schoolteacher deal with small, young rascals and constantly train new people to become bishops and councils, whenever it is necessary. A council prunes the large limbs from the tree or extirpates evil trees. But a pastor and a schoolteacher plant and cultivate young trees and useful shrubs in the garden. Oh, they have a precious office and task, and they are the church's richest jewels; they preserve the church. Therefore all the lords should do their part to preserve pastors and schools. For if indeed we cannot have councils, the parishes and schools, small though they are, are eternal and useful councils. (Luther, 1995, pp. 134-35)

He observed that education had originally been the primary task of the monasteries.

One can see quite well how earnestly the ancient emperors regarded parishes and schools [see the educational reforms of Charlemagne], since they endowed the monasteries so richly. That they were primarily schools is evidenced by these names: provost, dean, scholasticus, cantor, canonici, vicars, custodians, etc. But what has become of these? O Lord God! If they were at least willing to do something, remain what they were, keep what they had, were princes and lords, and again introduced hours of study and compelled the canons, vicars, and choir pupils to listen to a daily lesson from Holy Scripture so that they would again, in some sense, look like a school, and so that one could have pastors and bishops and thus help to rule the church. (Luther, 1995, p. 135)

There were other tasks that Luther envisioned being taken up by the schools, especially in the matter of ceremonies.

Ceremonies ought to be completely disregarded by the councils and should be left at home in the parishes, indeed, in the schools so that the schoolmaster, along with the pastor, would be "master of ceremonies" [*Magister Ceremonium*]. All others will learn these from the students, without any effort or difficulty. For instance, the common people will learn from the pupils what, when, and how to sing or pray in church; they will also learn what to sing by the bier or at the grave. When the pupils kneel and fold their hands as the schoolmaster beats time with his baton during the singing of "And was made man," the common people will imitate them. When they doff their little hats or bend their knees whenever the name of Jesus Christ is mentioned, or other Christian discipline and gestures they may exercise, the common people will do afterward without instruction, moved by the living example. (Luther, 1995, p. 136-137)

At the end of the second part of this treatise, Luther concluded that the church must do without a true council, and proposed what must be done instead.

Well then, if we must despair of a council let us commend the matter to the true judge, our merciful God. Meanwhile we shall promote the small and the young councils, that is, parishes and schools, and propagate St Peter's article [Acts 15:10-11] in every way possible, preserving it against all the accursed new articles of the faith and of the new good works with which the pope has flooded the world. (Luther, 1995, p. 142)

As Luther came to the end of the third and final section of his treatise "On Councils and the Church," in which he took up the doctrine of the church and its marks, he addressed also the place of schools in the church.

Above and elsewhere I have written much about the schools, urging firmness and diligence in caring for them. Although they may be viewed as something external and pagan, in as much as they instruct boys in languages and the arts, they are nevertheless extremely necessary. For if we fail to train pupils we will not have pastors and preachers very long—as we are finding out. The school must supply the church with persons who can be made apostles, evangelists, and prophets, that is, preachers, pastors, and rulers, in addition to other people needed throughout the world, such as chancellors, councilors, secretaries, and the like, men who can also lend a hand with the temporal government. In addition, if the schoolteacher is a godly man and teaches the boys to understand, to sing, and to practice God's word and the true faith and holds them to Christian discipline, then, as we said earlier, the schools are truly young and eternal councils, which perhaps do more good than many other great councils. Therefore the former emperors, kings, and princes did well when they showed such diligence in building many schools, high and low, monastic schools and convents, to provide the church with a rich and ample supply of people; but their successors shamefully perverted their use. Thus today princes and lords should do the same, and use the possessions of the cloisters for the maintenance of schools and provide many persons with the means for study. If our descendants misuse these, we at least have done our duty in our day.

In summary, the schools must be second in importance only to the church, for in them young preachers and pastors are trained, and from them emerge those who replace the ones who die.

Next, then, to the school comes the burgher's house, for it supplies the pupils; then the city hall and the castle, which must protect the schools so that they may train children to become pastors, and so that these, in turn, may create churches and children of God (whether they be burghers, princes, or emperors). (Luther, 1995, p. 176)

There is one final glimpse at Luther's thought on schooling, one that is of a personal nature. In 1542 Luther sent his son John, age 16, to the highly respected Torgau Latin School, where he was to stay with the headmaster, Marcus Crodel. Some details of the arrangement are unclear, for John had already received a bachelor's degree. Perhaps his father believed his education to be insufficient. Luther wrote,

Grace and peace! As you and I have agreed, my Marcus, I am sending my son John to you so that you may add him to the boys who are to be drilled in grammar and music. Also, keep an eye on his conduct and correct it, for in the Lord I have great confidence in you. I shall liberally pay for your expenses, and you will please inform me how much he has progressed in [a certain] time, and how much one might expect of him. I have added the boy Florian [son of Katherine's brother, who died in 1542], especially since I see that these boys need the example set by a crowd of many boys; this seems to me to accomplish more than individual, private education. But be very strict with this one, and if you can place him with a citizen, do it; otherwise send him back. May God prosper what has been begun.

If I see success with this son, then soon, if I live, you will also have my other two sons [Martin, 10, and Paul, 9]. For I think that after you there will be no teachers as diligent as you, especially in grammar and in strictness so far as conduct is concerned. Therefore "make use of the moment, for time races with a swift foot" [Ovid, *De arte amandi iii.65*], and diligent teachers disappear even faster. Thereafter the boys will return here for higher studies for which they will then be better equipped.

Farewell in the Lord, and tell John Walther [well-known Kantor of Torgau] that I pray for his well-being, and that I commend my son to him for learning music. For I, of course, produce theologians, but I also would like to produce grammarians and musicians. (Luther, 1995, vol. 50, pp. 231-32, Letter 296)

The need to produce theologians, grammarians, musicians, and the competent incumbents of all kinds of vocations is as great today for church, city, and home as it has ever been. The quotations and works of Luther cited above give excellent guidance for the formation of genuinely Lutheran, parish schools—schools that may well be called "classical" in the sense of the ancient and medieval liberal arts. Luther's words here do not give all the answers to many of the details of this education, nor indeed to the manner of its application in a world which has changed greatly since his day. The true foundation for the training of Christian children and youth will be found not in Luther's writing on education, but in the doctrine which he and we both confess. For there alone, in the doctrine of Holy Scriptures, can we decisively perceive that children have not changed from that day to this, nor the nature of knowledge or learning or understanding, nor the orders and institutions of God among men, nor the basic abilities of those who are needed for these orders and institutions. The same sins of children, parents, society and church institutions plague us. The same forgiveness and Gospel gifts must be the remedy to our ills. In our schools, the Holy Scriptures must continue to reign supreme in all its truth and purity.

———————————

The Reverend John Hill is pastor and headmaster of CCLE-accredited Mount Hope Lutheran School in Casper, Wyoming. Writer and speaker for CCLE, he has previously served as Board member of the Consortium for Classical and Lutheran Education.

## Classical Lutheran Education for Any Child

*by Cheryl Swope*

> For thousands of years, the classical arts of learning were the standard for education....The Good, the True, and the Beautiful were the objects of this sort of education... (Consortium for Classical Lutheran Education website, 7/09).

Some parents and educators have the misconception that classical education is only for "smart kids." It is not difficult to understand why someone might think this way. Latin at age 8? Herodotus by 14? With such standards, one might reason, surely classical education is only for born geniuses – the brightest and best of our children. Certainly for advanced performance at the highest levels of classical study, this theory has some merit. But what about those children who are not born geniuses? What about those who, far from being intellectually gifted, are living with cognitive challenges, language disorders, or physical disabilities? Does classical education have anything to offer them? Can classical education benefit any child?

No doubt Helen Keller's concerned parents asked the same question back in 1887. Their young daughter was deaf, blind, and severely "behaviorally disordered." Distraught and fearful for the little girl's future, as most parents would be, the Kellers hoped that Helen might somehow receive an education. In the late 1800's, this meant a classical education. Helen Keller began her adapted classical education at the age of six with her private teacher Annie Sullivan. Although no one could predict the eventual outcome, the Keller family embarked on this ambitious, beautiful journey nonetheless. And the world received captivating evidence that classical education truly can benefit any child.

In her later adult years, Helen Keller departed in some ways from the philosophies of classical Western civilization, but her story remains an important one as we explore how classical education can benefit any child. After all, Helen Keller's education more than a century ago mirrors the classical education of today. As soon as language unlocked Helen's young mind, Annie Sullivan taught Helen the same academic content other classically-educated children learn, but through patient, untiring finger-spelling into Helen's hand. From ages 8-10, Helen studied Geography and History. She read of Greek heroes and the classical ancient civilizations. She enjoyed beautiful language through good literature. She read poetic selections from the Old and New Testaments, *Lamb's Tales from Shakespeare*, Dickens' *A Child's History of England, Little Women, Heidi, The Swiss Family Robinson,* and countless other books which could still be found on the library shelves of any classical school today. Helen treasured her books: "I accepted them as we accept the sunshine and the love of our friends." (Keller, 1905, p. 105)

From the ages of 11-13, Helen learned Latin from a Latin scholar and French in raised print. She studied more advanced histories of Greece, Rome, and the United States, as Annie continued to spell lessons into Helen's hand. By age 16, Helen read works in the original Latin and German, and at age 20 she enrolled at Radcliffe where she read literature in French, studied World History, read poetry critically, and learned advanced English composition.

Helen's only real academic failure came when she was 17. One of her teachers made some common errors with this special-needs child, mistakes which continue to be made in many educational settings today. First, the teacher determined that Helen must devote herself only to those areas in which she was weakest, namely physics, algebra, and geometry. Moreover, he taught these subjects in a large classroom without necessary modifications. (For example, he wrote visual geometry proofs on the board with no means for Helen to follow along.) As a result, Helen required additional instruction with a tutor before she could enter Radcliffe as previously planned.

Looking back over her education, Helen later wrote, "From the storybook Greek Heroes to the Iliad [read in Greek] was no day's journey, nor was it altogether pleasant. One could have traveled round the world many times while I trudged my weary way through the labyrinthine mazes of grammars and dictionaries...." (Keller, 1905, p. 93) Helen received a remarkable classical education, because her parents and her teachers bonded together to help her, and she persevered. Although her disabilities remained with her all her life, so did her love for literature: "When I read the finest passages of the Iliad, I am conscious of a soul-sense that lifts me above the narrow, cramping circumstances of my life. My physical limitations are forgotten - my world lies upward, the length and the breadth and the sweep of the heavens are mine!" (Keller, 1905, p. 117)

If classical education could give Helen Keller the tools to overcome great obstacles and embrace the "sweeps of the heavens" so many years ago, why do even less-severely handicapped special-needs children fail to receive such a bountiful classical education today? Largely, the answer is simply historical timing. At the turn of the century, as special education grew in acceptance, classical education began to wane. In the 1930's, "the height of classical study in the United States in sheer numbers," nearly one million students studied Latin annually. By the 1970's, so-called *progressive*[4] and experimental education dominated. About this same time, just as classical education had all but disappeared, the landmark special education legislation Public Law 94-142 passed in the United States. This law mandated public education for all handicapped children. Public, yes, but often much less effective and far less beautiful.

Today, much of "regular education" has strayed so far from the pursuit of that which is significantly true, good, and beautiful, many special-needs or struggling children who have been placed in remedial or even age-based classrooms receive little that is inspiring, excellent, or formative. In the past, even "basic" education meant purposeful instruction in the three arts of language: Grammar – including reading, Latin, spelling, penmanship, and composition; Logic – analysis, reasoning, and discernment; and Rhetoric – persuasive eloquence in both speaking and writing. A good liberal arts education also included the four arts of mathematics: Arithmetic (number), Geometry (number in space), Music (number in time), and Astronomy (number in space and time). These seven liberal arts developed the mind and provided the student with essential tools for learning. Intrinsic to his learning, the student also studied history, good literature, and art, all for the formation of a strong mind and noble character. He applied his intellectual skills to the three branches of knowledge: the moral, natural, and theological sciences. Throughout the centuries, Christian catechesis - teaching the Christian faith - has also been urged alongside the liberal arts and sciences to address essential matters of the soul.

Instead, today the ideal in special education is "individualized instruction, in which the child's characteristics, rather than prescribed academic content, provide the basis for teaching techniques." (Hallahan et al., 2003, p. 24) Worse, in some special education teacher-training programs, not only progressivism and pragmatism, but also fatalistic, dehumanizing behaviorism dominates. The child's mind and soul are forgotten.

---

[4] "I believe, therefore, that the true center of correlation on the school subject is not science, nor literature, nor history, nor geography, but the child's own social activities." John Dewey, My Pedagogic Creed, Article III, (New York, E. L. Kellogg & Co., 1897), p. 10.

The special-needs child's humanity – *any child's humanity* – must determine the education he receives. Some suggest that as many as 1 in 5 children have special educational needs. Each of these children is a *human being*, created in the image of God. Shall we assign all of these students to a menial, servile education and deny them the riches of a beautiful, humane, liberating education? And, worse, shall we base our deterministic placements on early testing, with no regard to what the child might be able to overcome with the aid of an excellent teacher?

Quintilian wrote, "There is no foundation for the complaint that only a small minority of human beings have been given the power to understand what is taught them, the majority being so slow-witted that they waste time and labor. On the contrary, you will find the greater number quick to reason and prompt to learn. This is natural to man....Dull and unteachable persons...have been very few. The proof of this is that the promise of many accomplishments appears in children, and when it fades with age, this is plainly due to the failure not of nature but of care. 'But some have more talent than others.' I agree: then some will achieve more and some less, but we never find one who has not achieved something by his efforts." (Quintilian, Book 1:1)

Regardless of his challenges, any child is called to do more than receive services; he is called to love and serve his neighbor. Even if he is never able to hold a full-time paying "job," classical education can help the special-needs child bring purpose, love, or comfort to his parents. He is a student with lessons to learn, teachers to respect, and parents to honor. He is a young man who holds the door for aging members of his congregation. She is the person who thoughtfully replenishes a dog's fresh water bowl while her neighbor is away at work. She is a sister, granddaughter, or niece, with the high calling of gracious and tender service, as God works through her for His loving purposes.

We see uniquely converging opportunities at this time in history. Information abounds on special-needs and struggling learners. Classical education enjoys a re-emergence in numerous and growing pockets, for the youngest children through university levels. Abundant resources now offer instruction in Latin, the history of ancient civilizations, the mathematical arts, and more, at every level and with any amount of repetition and practice the child needs. Teachers, homeschooling parents, tutors – anyone who seeks to teach *any* child – can find helpful curricula for adapting reading, composition, Greek, music theory, literature, logic, and rhetoric. Perhaps the child will eventually prove incapable of progressing to advanced levels in one area or in every area; however, if taught slowly, patiently and systematically, even those children who are identified with or suspected of having "special learning needs" can receive a substantial, elevating, and beautiful education.

Classical education can address *any child's* challenges and cultivate in him a lifelong appreciation for lasting Goodness, Truth, and Beauty. Modifications can help with behavioral and neurological difficulties, language and sensory challenges, specific learning disabilities, and even severe mental illnesses. Be encouraged. Any child can receive the great benefits of classical education: greater self-knowledge, timeless tools for learning, a more disciplined mind, a love of study, and a dedicated life of service. Classical education is a beautiful gift to your child, and he can say with Helen Keller, "My world lies upward, the length and the breadth and the sweep of the heavens are mine!"

---

Cheryl Swope, M.Ed., is author of *Simply Classical: A Beautiful Education for Any Child* from which this article is excerpted. She and her husband have homeschooled their adopted special-needs twins from infancy through high school with classical Lutheran education. She serves as editor of the Classical Lutheran Education Journal and Board Member for the Consortium for Classical and Lutheran Education.

## The Freedom Of Grace And The Bondage Of The Neighbor: The Paradox Of Christian Nurture

*by Dr. Steven A. Hein*

Although not a Lutheran, David Hicks eloquently described a fundamental paradox inherent in a classical Christian education particularly when viewed from a Lutheran perspective. Hicks described a pedagogical tension in an education that would seek simultaneously to equip young minds for *the world's fight and the soul's salvation.* (Hicks, 1999, p. 2) This description closely parallels the paradoxical character of the Christian's life in one of Luther's early but most profound essays, his *Treatise on Christian Liberty*, better known as *The Freedom of the Christian* (1520). In this essay Luther stated it this way: *A Christian is a perfectly free lord of all, subject to none. A Christian is a perfectly dutiful servant of all, subject to all.* (Luther, 1995, Vol. 31, p. 344)

The intent of this essay is to explore the central importance of these paradoxes and how they are so important. More than ever, parents and Servants of the Word need understand them for the nurture of our children with an education that is distinctly classical and Lutheran. And this is the education that they vitally need. In this interest, I would add another way of describing Luther's paradox that shapes the Christian's identity: the Christian life is characterized by living in *the Freedom of Grace and the Bondage of the Neighbor.*

On the one hand, a distinctively Lutheran education needs to nurture understanding and attitudes that are shaped by the faith into which we are baptized. That faith centrally proclaims a life of secured freedom, a freedom just to be the children of God enjoying life with our Creator for the sake of the grace of Christ. When it comes to securing and maintaining God's favor, when it comes to grappling with the gap between the people we are and the people we ought to be, when it comes to securing our own welfare, there is nothing for us to do, nothing to accomplish, nothing to perfect. We must teach that getting saved is a matter of our doing nothing.

The real offense of the Gospel as it addresses the soul's salvation is that it calls us to a ridiculously passive life, not unlike that of a beggar. Beggars lack the basic things that are needed to live. Moreover, should they be given what they need for life, they have nothing to offer in return. They just stand there - hat in hand - ready to receive again and again whatever they can get. It is recounted that Luther's last spoken words on his deathbed were: *We are all beggars, and that's the truth.* And so here is our task: to raise up young beggars who make it a habit simply to go - spiritual hat in hand - to the throne of grace and receive all the donated dignity and sustenance for life they can get from the bleeding charity of a crucified Christ. They are to learn how to have and maintain a spiritual appetite simply to receive from the bloody hands of Jesus, all that they are and all that they need for life today and every day. And as beggars, they are to do this with the clear conviction that they do not, nor will they ever, have anything to offer their Lord in return. And this is just how it ought to be. When God has His way with us, we passively grow in an awareness and appreciation of our poverty and His graciousness. We may experience our spiritual poverty by the inner workings of Law and the external events that bring *tentatio* - trial and temptation - but we grasp the graciousness of God by faith alone. We are to teach our children to enjoy a freedom from being obligated ever to do anything for God. As Luther so eloquently put it in his Heidelberg Theses: *The Law says "do this," and it is never done. Grace says "believe in this," and everything is done already.*[5] What Luther learned from the Apostle Paul is that we can live life under the Law, or we can live it under the Gospel. Under the Law, when all is said and done, there is always more to do. But under the Gospel, when all is believed about the promises of Christ, all is already done, and there is nothing left to do. And with nothing, you get everything. You are free. This is the grace by which we are saved, and it brings an outrageous freedom - that has God whispering to us what Gerhard Forde has called the hilarity of the Gospel: *what are you going to do now that you don't have to do anything.* (Forde, 1990, p. 33)

By the standards of the world and good old-fashioned religion - even that which often seeks to pass itself off as Christian - this is an understanding of grace that is both outrageous and hilarious. We get everything we need in our baptismal inheritance, even adoption into the royal family of His Son; yet we remain beggars. We become kings in the kingdom with the Lord Christ who also made His appearance to the shout of *hosannas* as a royal beggar.[6] That makes us royal beggars! Our God is a God who demands perfect righteousness; yet it is this God who gives us just what He demands in the righteousness of Christ, given in the sacred things to us, again and again. And here is another paradox about that righteousness: we are now perfectly sufficient in the righteousness of Christ, yet we always are in need of more. Royal beggars for life.

The freedom of the Gospel is God's wisdom, but it is usually seen as foolishness - religious foolishness - from the human perspective. With man's sense of justice, everybody gets what they deserve. With God's justice, everybody gets what they do not deserve. The righteous Christ receives the wrath of God and punishment for sin, and we wretched sinners receive mercy. For us, it is all about getting saved, doing nothing. From the human standpoint, it sounds like a con job to keep us uncaring and lazy. Worldly wisdom operates with the assumption that the more important the issues connected with human existence, the more we need to get busy. The more God commands us, and He certainly commands us in His Law (they are not the Ten Suggestions!), the busier we think we need to be. Man's religion always advances the notion that there is Divine help for those who help themselves; thus, the apex of spiritual commitment is manifested in what we do. But against such a sensible perspective, we must teach our children to understand and appreciate the divine foolishness of the Gospel which operates with different logic. The Gospel teaches, ironically, what is contrary to what well-meaning Christian parents often teach, especially around Christmas time: *tis better to give than to receive.* The logic of the Gospel, however, is just the reverse: *tis better to receive than to give.* We must teach that all commitments to giving produce just what Aristotle promised: a growth in worldly virtues; but, when it comes to the soul's salvation, when such things are trusted in, they also produce a ticket to Hell. Conversely, the passive reception of the saving gifts of Christ produce just what the Apostle Paul promised: a perfect righteousness and a ticket to Heaven.

Our challenge, today more than ever before, is to provide the experiences, vantage points, and the theological logic by which our children can see (first of all) and then appreciate (second of all) the

---

[5] *Heidelberg Disputation*, 1518, Thesis 26, AE, 31:41.

[6] Our royal beggarly identity flows, in part, from our union and inheritance with Christ, whose royal reign was hidden under a beggarly appearance. Luther refers to Jesus as the royal beggar as he expounds on Matthew's connection with the prophecy of Zechariah 9:9 concerning His triumphal, yet humble, entry into Jerusalem. "He rides there so beggarly, but hearken to what is said and preached about this poor king. His wretchedness and poverty are manifest, for He comes riding on an ass like a beggar having neither saddle nor spurs. But that He will take from us sin, strangle death, endow us with eternal holiness, eternal bliss, and eternal life, this cannot be seen. Wherefore thou must hear and believe." WA 37:201-202 as cited in David Steinmetz, Luther in Context (Grand Rapids: Baker Book House, 1995), p. 28.

freedom that the grace of Christ imparts. In this regard, Christian pedagogy for our children has often made a critical mistake - one that, unfortunately, has been passed on for generations. We think that life in Christ can best be nurtured and appreciated by our small children through engaging their hands in meaningless handicrafts and their minds in unnecessarily watered-down Bible stories. We then mix this formula with bland thoughts about a milk-toast love of Jesus for bunnies and butterflies. We have witnessed how this regimen of soft religious pabulum produces mischievous boredom in our strong-willed boys by age 8 and utter rebellion by many of both sexes by age 13. In the eyes of these children, the youth culture of today may not be seen as very wholesome, but it certainly is not so boring!

We need to recover the distinctively Lutheran understanding on how hearts and minds are prepared for the Gospel. We must renew our faith in what Professor Ronald Feuerhahn has called *the power of negative thinking*.[7] The power of negative thinking is harnessed by frequent sojourns in the way of full-strength Law. Spiritual Beggars are made - and renewed in their passion to beg - by a continual experience of their own spiritual poverty. Only those who die to sin may live in Christ. This is as true for the two - and three-year-old baptized as it is for their parents.

The theological logic that anchors the freedom of the Gospel entails three very important adversaries that must be overcome: sin, death, and the Devil. Without a real awareness and appreciation of these three enemies, the foolishness of the Gospel will be simply foolishness, and progressively uninteresting foolishness at that. We must continually expose our children to these evils in their own life and world in order to nurture and maintain a beggar's mindset for life. Sin has rendered our little children dead in their trespasses, prone to make idols out of most anything or anyone, and curved in upon themselves with inordinate self-love. As with all of us - to use the botanical metaphor - they have become bad vines in a bad vineyard, producing nothing but sour grapes.[8] We are and remain in this life - apart from Christ - wretched sinners.

One of the biggest challenges for the Christian nurture of our young people is to make these realities clear, important, concrete, and related to the fabric of how life must be lived in a fallen world. The freedom to live as beggars of God's favor in Christ Jesus - with the peace and security that this brings - makes little sense apart from an awareness and appreciation of the magnitude of the problem of evil. For this the Law needs to have more than its instruction; it needs to have its effect. The power of negative thinking needs to have an impact in the lives of our children early and often, not just for discipline, but also for appropriate character formation. The problem of sin needs not simply to be instructed; it needs to be experienced. The power of negative thinking is the conviction in the hearts of our children by the work of the Spirit that they can die to sin. . . or they can just die. This conviction is what creates a passionate life of begging for God's outrageous grace, trusting to exercise the freedom of the Gospel to receive the riches of God's grace without any concern over the issue of what they might give in return. For them, as for each of us, they can live by grace or they won't live at all.

But thanks be to God, they will live by grace. The awareness of the riches of God's grace may be no greater than the awareness of the magnitude of one's sin. Our children can only grasp the wonder of the way of the Gospel as it is balanced by the impact of the Law. They will make progress maturing in the image of Christ bit by bit, as Luther put it, by always starting over again - dying to sin in the way of

---

[7]The Rev., Dr. Ronald Feuerhahn has been a faithful and stimulating professor of Systematic Theology at Concordia Seminary, St. Louis, MO for many years.

[8]An allusion to the metaphor in Isaiah 5:1-4.

the Law and rising up unto new life in the freedom of the Gospel. (Luther, 1995, Vol. 25, p. 478) This is as true for our little ones as it is for our teenagers, as it is for each of us.

Now at this point you may have been thinking *but. . . but. . . but you are leaving things out, important things!* Yes, that is true. There is another side of the life of the Christian. The freedom of grace we have covered. But now we must turn our attention to the other side of the paradox: the bondage of the neighbor. We must prepare our children for what Hicks calls *the world's fight*. Christians are simultaneously free and bound. Strangely, the notions of freedom and slavery are not always opposites from a biblical perspective. In the civil sphere, our forefathers closely linked the idea of freedom with the idea of liberty, that is self-government or autonomous self-rule. Our Declaration of Independence declared that we would be a free people, determined to govern ourselves, independent from the British Crown. However, when the Scriptures address what Luther called things above us - spiritual matters - they know nothing of human autonomy. We are either ruled at all points by the powers and principalities of evil or we are ruled by God.[9] The Scriptures do not tie the notion of freedom to autonomy; rather, they tie the idea of freedom to purpose - God's purposes. The Christian's life is free, and yet it is a life of slavery. Yes, Jesus taught that *if the Son has set you free, you will be free indeed*.[10] But He also instructed His disciples that as they rightly acknowledged Him as Lord, this meant that they are slaves, *doulos*; and a slave is not above his master.[11] In the same vain, the Apostle Paul explained that in our Baptism, we have been set free from the slavery of sin and are alive to God in Christ Jesus. But we have also thereby become slaves to God and to righteousness.[12] As slaves are bound to their master, so we are bound to Christ. We are a new creation fashioned after His human nature and created for the works which God has planned from eternity that we should be about.[13]

The sense of bondage here involves a necessary connection between our being and our doing. When it comes to spiritual things, we do as we are. Good fruit comes from a good tree as bad fruit from a bad tree. Grapes come from grapevines because that is how God has made them. Jesus taught that He is the vine and we the branches and that abiding in Him we can produce some pretty good vintage. What we do flows from what we are. It is God Who has so connected our being and doing. There is freedom here, for this is how God has designed us to be, but it is not autonomy. This again is Aristotle on his head. Aristotle taught that we are perfected in our being by a progressive perfecting of what we do. *Doing* is an investment in *becoming* - for good or ill. For this reason, Luther saw Aristotle's *Nichomachian Ethics* as of the Devil, for it runs counter to the whole sense of the creating and saving work of God.

Luther observed in his Heidelberg Theses that *the love of God does not find, but creates that which is pleasing to it*. (Luther, 1995, Vol. 31, p. 41) God never comes to us as a beggar - hat in hand - hoping to get from us what He desires. (For example, God really would like you to become a Christian. How

---

[9]This means that in Christ we are bound to His righteousness which produces the fruit of faith; and apart from Christ, we are bound to sin. Luther used the unflattering illustration of a mule who is ridden by its master in this regard. In spiritual matters we are as a mule, either ridden by the Devil or we are ridden by Christ. Oberman's discussion of "man as a mule" is a delightful explanation of Luther's analogy here. He writes: ". . . for Luther, man is not the mule that, stupefied by ignorance, cannot decide between two haystacks - education could help that mule. No the condition of man does not depend on the breadth of his education but on his existential condition as a 'mule' ridden either by God or the Devil, but with no choice in the matter, no freedom of decision, no opportunity for self-determination." Heiko Oberman, *Luther: Man between God and the Devil* (New York: Image Books, Doubleday, 1990), p.219.

[10]John 8:36.

[11]John 13:13-16.

[12]Romans 6:7, 17-19, 22.

[13]See Romans 5:17, Ephesians 2:10, 4:13-15.

about it? What do you say?) Whatever God wants, He just makes all by Himself. He needs no help from us. The general interpretive rubric for the Bible is this: whatever God commands, God creates. And whatever God demands, God gives. He commanded the creation of human beings in Genesis 1, and through the power of His Word, it was so. He demands of us a perfect righteousness in His Law, and He gives us just that in the righteousness of Christ through the Gospel. In the Gospel, He exhorts faith, and that is what He creates by the power of the Spirit through the Word of Christ.[14] His redemptive will is that we become a New Creation in Christ, and that is just what He fashions by the power of the saving Word in the waters of Baptism. We are as He has made and remade us; and we do as we are in accord with His will and work.

One would conclude that if God has regenerated us to be slaves of the Lord Jesus, then we must above all serve and be obedient to Him. Indeed, this is how much of the theology in the Church through the ages has seen it. The Christian has been called to a life bound by a higher calling, to perform special spiritual works for our Lord Jesus out of obedience to Him. The more pious you are, the more time you devote in your life to doing them. Such an idea flourished in medieval monasticism. You go to the monastery to perform super-spiritual works for your merit and for Christ's benefit. Today we see the remnants of such thinking even in our Lutheran congregations. We dream up special works to serve Jesus in our congregations and then we implore our members to come and do them on a regular basis. Congregations that can fill up a monthly calendar with such events are called *alive*. And those who busy themselves doing them are called *active members*. We call this congregational monasticism and it is a misunderstanding about Christian piety and works.[15]

To engage the world's fight is to leave the confines of monastery or church building and enlist your talents and energies in the temporal orders of life - to be of some earthly good. In the thinking of Luther, it is to make things in this life a little bit better. The Christian life proclaims a bondage to our neighbor and his welfare. We cannot serve our Lord Jesus directly for two rather unflattering reasons. The first is that we do not have anything that He needs. The second - equally unflattering - is that whatever we have that is worth anything, He gave us. Faith generates love. God would have us channel our fear, love, and trust in Him (things that are just part and parcel with being a new creation in Christ) distributing as stewards the blessings that God has entrusted to us. He binds our deeds to our neighbor and gives us some significant things to do in this life. At the same time, He schools us in the gentle art of loving - something that we shall be doing for an eternity. And then He makes this arrangement: serving the neighbor in faith is reckoned as service rendered to Him, even when that service is rendered to those one might consider the least of His brothers.[16]

The bondage of the neighbor is to be understood in a two-fold sense: in the way of the Gospel, and in the way of the Law. As a new creation in Christ, this bondage is composed of the compelling demands of gratitude and love. In the way of the Gospel, we serve the neighbor out of delightful gratitude for all that our Lord has done and given to us.[17] This is a bound freedom from all concerns about our own welfare as these are put to rest in the secured gifts and promises of Christ. Moreover, we serve our

---

[14]Romans 1:16, 10:17, I Corinthians 12:3.

[15]For a more complete discussion of the false piety exhibited in monasticism and contemporary congregational forms of the same thing, see my essay, "The Outer Limits of a Lutheran Piety," *LOGIA - A Journal of Lutheran Theology*, Vol. 3:1, January, 1994, 4-10.

[16]See Jesus' teaching about the works of the sheep on Judgment Day in Matthew 25:31-40.

[17]We serve out of a sense of loyalty to Christ who is Lord and has made us servant/slaves - not out of a sense of legal compulsion but by grace. The life of service flows from an ethos under grace, not law.

neighbor out of love, because that is just what the New Creation has been created to do. We are God's piece of work and we do as we are. These realities undergird the usually taught *because-you-want-to* side of things. This is the delightful bondage of love. The neighbor becomes a beloved, and it is love's compulsion to serve and bestow gifts for her welfare. Little Suzie falls down and skins her knees. Her loving mother picks her up, comforts her and tends to her wounds. Now should we be so silly as to ask the mother why she did this or if she thought she *had* to, she would surely think we were crazy. Works of love have a bondage about them - even a compulsion - as one is captivated by the needs of a beloved, but legal considerations of duty and calculation have no place.

Such is the bondage of the neighbor as the Christian, as seen in light of the realities of the New Creation in Christ brought forth from the waters of Baptism. There is another side to the bondage of the neighbor, because there is another side to the Christian. Apart from Christ, the Christian remains a fleshly sinner, sold as a slave to sin in which nothing good dwells and nothing good comes forth.[18] The bondage of the neighbor occasions for the Christian a context to carry on the subduing and disciplining of the flesh. Moreover, it is a significant hill on the battlefield where spiritual warfare is to be engaged against the world, the flesh, and the Devil. To our children we are to say, *you don't want to? . . . well you have to.* This is the bondage of the neighbor in the way of the Law.

We need to be very clear on this. There is no liberty in the bondage of the neighbor. There is no liberty in our doing or in the nurture of our children's doing. We can be constrained by the love of Christ and captivated by the needs of the neighbor, or we can be strained by the Law and serve our neighbor for our own good . . . or as is often the case, we can be constrained by both.[19] It is a win-win situation in either case. In the paradoxical nurture of our children that addresses the bondage of the neighbor, we are to use discipline with all its rewards and penalties to teach what *the fat relentless ego*[20] in all of our children needs to understand: life will go better for them if they follow the rules than if they break them. We call such service that flows from discipline *civil righteousness.* It is not intrinsically the stuff of godliness; it is the stuff of practical wisdom. So we teach our children: *do yourself a favor, follow the rules!*

A good tree bears what the Lord considers good fruit, and a bad tree bears what is considered bad fruit. But the Lord can use either or both to feed your neighbor quite sufficiently. Warming the heart of our children by the Gospel produces the bondage of love; and warming the butt of our children produces the disciple of the Law. . . or other such applications that get the message across. Both Law and Gospel are needed to nurture the bondage of the neighbor.

Nurturing children to live in the freedom of Grace and the bondage of the neighbor corresponds to a dual citizenship that God has called all of His Children to occupy as the Church Militant. Under the lordship

---

[18] See the Apostle Paul's description in Romans 7:14-20. Luther expressed this "you do as you are" understanding between faith and unbelief in the following way: "So it is with the works of man. As the man is, whether believer or unbeliever, so also is his work - good, if it was done in faith, wicked if it was done in unbelief. But the converse is not true, that the work makes the man either a believer or an unbeliever." AE, 31:361.

[19] Forde expressed this duality of motivation as rather typical of ordinary saints, and even more so. "To be realistic, this side of the eschaton we shall no doubt have to say that in our actual deeds there is something of a mixture of the *have* to and the *want* to, maybe even a good deal more of the former than the latter. But we must not loose sight of the hope, the vision, inspired by the absolutely unconditional promise. For in the end, that alone will survive - true sanctification." G. Forde, *Justification*, p. 57.

[20] A delightful term for the central enemy of moral life coined by Iris Murdoch. See her *The Sovereignty of Good* (London: Rutledge & Kegan Paul, 1970), pp. 52, 66.

of Christ, we are simultaneously citizens of the Kingdom of God and worldly earthly communities. We live a secure life as beggars of the grace that makes us free, and we live significant lives with works that bind us to our neighbors. These are great and wondrous truths about the fundamental identity of all of us, including our children - yes even the smallest of these. These children are simply on loan to us from their Heavenly Father and, through adoption, their Brother-in-Gospel. Let's put away the glitter, the finger painting, and the silly things that we do in the name of Christian education and teach this paradoxical identity of life in the Cross of Christ. Let us rightly divide the Word of Truth, teaching and applying God's law and His Gospel that our children might adopt a life-long habit of dying to live - dying to sin and rising unto newness of life, serving Christ in the neighbor's need - lords of all, beholding to none, yet servants of all and subject to all. Let us nurture our children with the goal and confident hope that in that day when you gather your earthly family together in the fullness of salvation, by the grace of God, they will be there.

---

Dr. Steven A. Hein (M.Div Concordia Theological Seminary, Master of Theology in Systematic Theology; PhD Historical Theology) teaches Theology and Apologetics as an affiliate faculty member with Patrick Henry College. Director of the Concordia Institute for Christian Studies and Founding Member of the Consortium for Classical and Lutheran Education, Dr. Hein speaks around the country on matters of classical Christian education, vocation, and faith-life in the Church and the world.

Notes

# References

Adams, J. (1851). *The works: 4 works, letters of Novanglus.* Little, Brown & Co, Boston.

Aristotle (1997). *Politics, in classic and contemporary readings in the philosophy of education.* McGraw Hill, New York.

Augustine (1995). *Augustine de doctrina christiana.* Oxford Press, New York.

Baldwin, T. W. (1944). *William Shakspere's small latine & lesse greeke.* University of Illinois Press, Illinois.

Bede (1968). *History of the english church and people.* Penguin, New York, trans leo sherley-price ed edition.

Bede (1999). *The ecclesiastical history of the english people.* Oxford University Press, Oxford.

Bede (2006). *Lutheran service book; A hymn of glory let us sing.* Concordia Publishing House, St. Louis.

Bederman, D. J. (2008). *The classical foundations of the American Constitution: Prevailing wisdom.* Cambridge University Press, Cambridge.

Bonner, S. F. (1977). *Education in ancient Rome: From the elder Cato to the younger Pliny.* University of California Press, Berkeley and Los Angeles, CA.

Brehaut, E. (1969). *Gregory of tours, history of the Franks.* Columbia University Press, New York, trans ed. edition.

Brown, P. (2007). *What's in a name? Opening of Oxford Centre for Late Antiquity,.* Oxford Centre For Late Antiquity, England.

Bukofzer, M. (1947). *Music in the Baroque Era.* W.W. Norton & Co., Inc., New York, NY.

Cahill, T. (1995). *How the Irish saved civilization.* Nan A. Talese/Doubleday, London.

Cassiodorus, Halporn, J. W., and Vessey, M. (2004). *Cassiodorus: Institutions of divine and secular learning and on the soul.* Liverpool University Press, Liverpool.

Cassiodorus and Walsh, P. G. (1990). *Cassiodorus, explanation of the Psalms.* Paulist Press, New York.

CCLE (2010). *Marks of a classical and Lutheran school.* The Consortium for Classical and Lutheran Education.

Chinard, G. (1933). *Honest John Adams.* Little, Brown, and Co., Boston.

Chinard, G. (1940). *Polybius and the American Constitution.* Journal of the History of Ideas, Inc, Philadelphia.

Compagni, D. (1986). *Dino Compagni's chronicle of Florence.* University of Pennsylvania Press, Philadelphia.

D'Aularie, I. and DAulaire, E. P. (1962). *Book of Greek myths.* Delacorte Press, New York, NY.

Dear, P. (2009). *Revolutionizing the sciences: European knowledge and its ambitions, 1500-1700.* Princeton UP, Princeton, 2nd edition.

Dewey, J. (2010). *Democracy and education.* Wilder Publications Ltd.

Dunne, J. (1993). *Back to the rough ground.* University of Notre Dame Press.

Edmundson, M. (1997). As lite entertainment for bored college students. *Harper's Magazine.*

Farrand, M. (1987). *The records of the Federal Convention of 1787: Vol. I.* Yale University Press, New Haven.

Forde, G. O. (1990). *Justification by faith: A matter of death and life.* Sigler Press, Ramsey, NJ.

Fuhrmann, M. (2002). *Bildung: Europas kulturelle identitt.* Stuttgart : Reclam, Germany.

Gatto, J. T. (1992). *Dumbing us down: The hidden cirriculum of compulsory schooling.* New Society Publishers, Gabriola Island, BC.

Gatto, J. T. (2001). *The underground history of American education: A schoolteacher's intimate investigation into the problem of modern schooling.* Oxford Village Press, New York.

Goldberg, S. A. (1966). *High school enrollments in latin 1964-65. Classical Bulletin,* volume 66.

Greeley, H. (2008). Towards responsible use of cognitive-enhancing drugs by the healthy. *Nature,* December 11:456, 702–705.

Groopman, J. (2002). Science fiction. *The New Yorker,* February 4.

Grout, Jay, D., and Palisca, C. V. (1960). *A history of Western music.* W.W. Norton & Co., Inc., New York, NY.

Gunton, C. (1985). *Enlightenment and alienation: An essay toward a trinitarian theology.* Wiff &Stock, Eugene. OR.

Haar, J. (2010). *Some introductory remarks on musical pedagogy. In music education in the Middle Ages and the Renaissance.* Indiana University Press, Bloomington, IN.

Hallahan, D. P., Kauffman, J. M., and Pullen, P. C. (2003). *Exceptional learners: Introduction to special education.* Boston, Allyn and Bacon.

Halsall, G. (2007). *The preface to book v of Gregory of tours' histories: Its form, context and significance,* volume Vol. CXXII. The English Historical Review.

Hamilton, A., Jay, J., Madison, J., and Rakove, J. N. (2003). *The federalist: The essential essays by Alexander Hamilton, James Madison and John Jay, with related documents.* u.a.: Bedford, Boston.

Handlin, O. (1979). *Truth in history.* Belknap PressHarvard, Cambridge, MA.

Herodotus (1890). *The history of Herodotus*, volume 1. MacMillan & Co, London & New York.

Hicks, D. V. (1999). *Norms and nobility: A treatise on education.* University Press of America, New York.

Jefferson, T. and Peterson, M. D. (1984). *Writings.* Literary Classics of the U.S., New York.

Jones, J. E., editor (2005). *Kitzmiller v. Dover area school district et al (Case No. 04cv2688).*

Joseph, S. M. and McGlinn, M. (2002). *The trivium, the liberal arts of logic, grammar, and rhetoric : Understanding the nature and function of language.* Paul Dry Books, Inc, Philadelphia.

Keller, H. (1905). *The story of my life.* Grosset and Dunlap, New York.

Kline, M. (1953). *Mathematics in Western culture.* Oxford University Press, New York.

Kolb, R. and Wengert, T. J., editors (2000). *The book of concord: The confessions of the Evangelical Lutheran Church.* Fortress Press, Minneapolis.

Korcok, T. (2011). *Lutheran education: From Wittenberg to the future.* Concordia Publishing House, St. Louis.

Kristol, I. (2011). *Encounter in the neo-conservative persuasion: Selected essays 1942-2009.* Basic Books, New York.

Laistner, M. L. W. (1933). *Bede as a classical and a patristic scholar*, volume 16 of *4th.* Transactions of the Royal Historical Society.

Latimer, J. F. (1958). *What's happened to our high schools?* Public Affairs Press, Washington, D.C.

Lennox, J. (2007). *Gods undertaker: Has science buried God.* Wilkinson House, Oxford.

Leppin, V. (2010). *Martin luther.* Darmstadt : WBG (Wissenschaftliche Buchgesellschaft), Germany.

Levin, Y. (2008). *The confused congresswoman.* The New Atlantis.

Lewis, C. S. (1952). *Voyage of the dawn treader.* MacMillan Co, New York.

Lewis, C. S. (1964, 2004). *The discarded image.* University Press, Cambridge, 9th edition.

Littlejohn, R. and Evans, C. (2006). *Wisdom and eloquence: A Christian paradigm for classical learning.* Crossway Books, Wheaton, Illinois.

Luther, M. (1955). *Luther: Letters of spiritual council.* John Knox Press, Westminster.

Luther, M. (1955-1995). *Luther's works: The American edition*, volume 1-55. Concordia Publishing House and Fortress Press, St. Louis.

Luther, M. (1960). *Preface to Galeatius Capellas history. Luthers works: Career of the reformer IV.* Fortress Press, Philadelphia.

Luther, M. (1988). *Luther's large catechism.* Concordia Publishing House.

Luther, M. (1991). *Small catechism with explanation.* Concordia Publishing House, St. Louis.

Madison, J. (1867). *Letters and other writings of James Madison, fourth President of the United States.* J.B. Lippincott, Philadelphia.

Martineau, J. (2010). *Quadrivium: The four classic liberal arts of number, geometry, music and cosmology.* Walker & Company, New York, NY.

Mayhew, J. (1766). *The snare broken: A thanksgiving-discourse.* R. & S. Draper, in Newbury-Street; Edes & Gill, in Queen-Street; and T. & J. Fleet, in Cornhill, Boston.

Miriam, J. and McGlinn, M. (2002). *The trivium: The liberal arts of logic, grammar, and rhetoric: Understanding the nature and function of language.* Paul Dry Books, Philadelphia, PA.

Murphy, James J. A Short History of Writing Instruction. Hermagoras Press: Davis, C. . p. . (1990). *A short history of writing instruction.* Hermagoras Press, Davis, CA.

Murray, R. E. (2010). *Zacconi as teacher: A pedagogical style in words and deeds. In music education in the middle ages and the renaissance.*

Newman, J. (2005). *On the scope and nature of university education.* Cosimo, Inc., New York.

Newman, J. H. C. (1982). *The idea of a university.* University of Notre Dame Press.

Nickel, J. (2001). *Mathematics: Is God silent?* Ross House Books, Vallectio, California 95251.

Numbers, R. L. (2009). *Galileo goes to jail, and other myths about science and religion.* Harvard University Press, Cambridge.

Oberby, P. J. (2005). The moral education of doctors. *The New Atlantis,* Fall.

Pesce, D. (2010). *Guido DArezzo, ut queant laxis, and musical understanding. In music education in the middle ages and the renaissance.* Indiana University Press, Bloomington, IN.

Plato and Jowell (2000). *The republic.* Dover Publications, Mineola, NY.

Postman, N. (1990). Informing ourselves to death. Stuttgart, Germany. Gesellschaft fuer informatik (German Informatics Society).

Quintilian. *The Institutio oratoria of Quintilian,* volume I. G. P. Putnams's Sons, New York.

Raleigh, W. (1938). *Preface to the history of the world. Prefaces and prologues to famous books.* P.F. Collier & Son, New York.

Richard, C. J. (2009). *The golden age of the classics in America: Greece, Rome, and the antebellum United States.* Harvard University Press, Cambridge, Mass.

Rossiter, C. (1953). *Seedtime of the republic: The origin of the American tradition of political liberty.* Harcourt, Brace, New York.

Rush, B. and Butterfield, L. H. (1951). *Letters of Benjamin Rush.* Princeton University Press, Princeton.

Sayers, D. (1947). The lost tools of learning.

Shafer, R. J., editor (1975). *A guide to historical method.* Dorsey Press, Homewood, IL.

Southern, R. W. (1970). *Aspects of the European tradition of historical writing: The classical tradition from Einhard to Geoffrey of Monmouth,* volume 191 of 5. Transactions of the Royal Historical Society.

Spivey, N. and Squire, M. (2004). *Panorama of the classical world.* Thames 8 Hudson Ltd, London.

Thorpe, L. (1988). *Einhard and notker the stammerer, two lives of charlemagne.* Penguin Books, trans ed edition.

Veith, G. E. (2002). *God at work: Your christian vocation in all of life.* Crossway Books, Wheaton, Illinois.

Veith, G. E. (2011). *Vocation in education. In learning at the foot of the cross: A lutheran vision for education.* Concordia University Press, Austin, TX.

Veith, G. E. and Kern, A. (2001). *Classical education: The movement sweeping America.* Capital Research Center, Washington, DC.

Wagner, D. L. (1983). *The seven liberal arts in the Middle Ages.* Indiana University Press, Bloomington.

Westman, R. S. (1975). *The Melanchthon circle, rheticus, and the Wittenberg interpretation of the Copernican Theory. Isis,* volume 66.

Winterer, C. (2002). *The culture of classicism: Ancient Greece and Rome in American intellectual life, 1780-1910.* Johns Hopkins University Press, Baltimore.

Made in the USA
Columbia, SC
02 February 2021

32167460R00096